All Scripture references taken from the KJV of the Holy Bible, unless otherwise indicated.

Mad At Daddy: How Father-Wounds Shape Motherhood & How God Heals Them,

by Dr. Marlene Miles

Freshwater Press, USA

ISBN: 978-1-967860-82-1 Paperback Version

ISBN: 978-1-967860-74-6 eBook Version

Table of Contents

MAD AT DADDY

How Father-Wounds Shape Motherhood & How God Heals Them

Foreshuvalen

✒ Introduction

When Anger Travels Through Generations

Most women never realize they are carrying anger. Not the loud kind. Not the dramatic kind. Not the kind that breaks dishes or raises voices. I'm talking about the kind that settles into the bones. The kind that hides behind responsibility. The kind that shows up only when life slows down long enough to feel it.

And for many women, that hidden anger doesn't begin with the child—it begins with the father of the child--the man who left. The man who disappointed. The man who changed. The man who promised more than he gave. The man who was never really present—not emotionally, not spiritually, sometimes not physically at all. And especially if that man is in a known place, doing what he should be doing for the mother and his child for or with someone else and not them. This may be the pain of all pains—the emotional pain of all emotional pains.

But the anger aimed toward a man cannot always land on him. So, it travels. It shifts. It transfers. It leaks out in the places where a woman feels the least defended—often in her own home, toward the children she loves but who unknowingly carry his face, his DNA, his absence, his memory, or his mistakes.

This is not because mothers are cruel. It is because mothers are human. And human beings tend to pour out whatever fills them, especially when they are tired, overwhelmed, or navigating life alone.

This book is not an accusation. It is not a judgment on mothers, single or married. It is not a condemnation of women who have done the best they could with the tools they had. This book is a mirror—not to shame, but to heal. A revealing—not to blame, but to restore. A compassionate excavation—not just to expose wounds, but to finally close and heal them.

Most mothers would never intentionally harm their child emotionally. But unhealed pain has a way of creating shadows in the heart—shadows that shape tone, reaction, expectation, affection, and connection. When a woman carries scars from the father, often without realizing it, those scars speak louder than her heart's actual intentions. They speak in sighs, in impatience, in distance, in frustration, in sharp words, in emotional withdrawal.

Here is the good news: **God never leaves a wound untouched when a mother is willing to be healed.** He never leaves or forsakes not even one of us. He never abandons a family that invites Him in.

He never lets generational patterns continue once they're named and surrendered.

This book is the beginning of that surrender. A journey to understand what's been happening in the spiritual and emotional background. A path toward inner healing, maternal restoration, and legacy transformation. Not because mothers are the problem, but because mothers carry the heart of the home, and when her heart is healed, the whole house begins to breathe again.

CHAPTER 1

When a Mother Hurts, a Child Feels It

A woman doesn't have to speak her pain for her home to hear it. Her emotions create the atmosphere. Her internal world becomes the climate. Her unspoken wounds become the undercurrent that everyone feels without ever naming.

Children especially.

Children have a way of sensing emotional weather long before they can understand it. They read tone like adults read facial expressions. They interpret silence the way adults interpret words. Children don't need explanations to feel distance. They don't need details to feel tension. They don't need the story to feel the storm.

When a mother hurts, a child feels it—even when the child has nothing to do with the source of that hurt. And for many women, the source is old. Older than the child. Older than the breakup. Older than the pregnancy. Older than motherhood itself.

It is the unresolved ache from the father of the child—an ache that was covered, ignored, minimized, or pushed aside in order to survive.

Women are strong. Women are resilient. Women are capable of moving forward while bleeding emotionally, sometimes silently, sometimes out loud. But emotional bleeding has symptoms. It shows up in shorter patience, quicker irritation, deeper exhaustion, unexplained resentment, emotional detachment, projection, overprotectiveness, or the opposite — disengagement. Not because she's a bad mother— but because she is a hurting woman.

And when a woman hurts, she becomes divided. Part of her is mother. Part of her is daughter. Part of her is still the woman who loved that man. Part of her is still the woman who was disappointed by him. These parts don't always agree. They don't always heal at the same pace. They don't always react the same way.

So, when the child cries, asks for attention, needs help, or simply exists that may bring a reaction from the mother. That child whose only crime may be having the father's face, voice, or some other trait which may bring a response from the woman's unhealed parts, instead of her healed ones. The child doesn't understand this. The mother doesn't always realize it. But the home can feel it. This is quite unfair really because a mother where the father is not there is to heal physically and emotionally from childbirth, nurture a child and run everything in the

9

house or all that is around her at the same time. *Alone?* This is tough for even a superwoman.

This is why healing matters. Not because a woman is doing anything intentionally harmful— but because her heart deserves to live without weight, without wounds, without those echoes of disappointment that spill into motherhood.

The child is not the wound. The child is not the memory. The child is not the father. The child is an assignment from God. A soul that is given both for and with purpose. The child is a life designated with divine identity. But when a mother's heart is tired, heavy, or unhealed, she may not see the child clearly— not because she doesn't love the child, but because her vision is being filtered through old injuries she never chose and never wanted.

This book is not to expose the mother—

it is to free her.

Once a woman understands where her reactions come from, she can separate her pain from her child, her disappointment from her motherhood, her past from her present. When that separation begins, the healing begins. And when the healing begins, the mother returns to herself—whole, present, loving, and free.

CHAPTER 2

The Invisible Tie to the Father

Why a Woman's Heart Toward the Man Shapes Her Heart Toward the Child

Most women don't realize it, but however you feel about the father, you may eventually feel something akin to it about the child. Not the same thing. Not the same intensity. Not the same reason, but a residue. An echo. A subtle emotional impression that transfers without permission. This is not sin. This is not failure. This is human nature plus spiritual dynamics.

When a child enters the world, they enter with two biological cords:

1. **the one God used to connect them to the mother,** and

2. **the one life uses to connect them to the father**.

That second cord is invisible but powerful. It holds the memories, emotions, disappointments, hopes, heartbreaks, and expectations a mother once had toward the man. Even if the child was born after the relationship ended, even if the mother has "moved on," even if the father is absent or unknown—the emotional cord remains until healing breaks it.

Not the cord of biology. Not the cord of responsibility. The cord of **unresolved emotion.**

Here's the painful truth that nobody talks about: the emotional carryover. Unprocessed feelings toward a man rarely stay with the man. They travel to the closest, safest target, and tragically, that is usually the child. This is not on purpose, not consciously, not with malice. It happens the same way a person limps after spraining an ankle— the body is compensating. The heart compensates too. When a woman has unresolved emotions toward the father, the child becomes a reminder, a symbol, a representation, a continuation, a reflection, a trigger, a provocation, a mirror she didn't ask for. This does not mean she loves the child any less. In fact, the love often makes the tension more confusing. She loves the child deeply, but the child also carries the shadow of the man who hurt her, left her, failed her, or disappointed her.

So, when she looks at the child, she may see his eyes, his attitude, his DNA, his mannerisms, his stubbornness, his humor, or simply his existence. And her heart gets pulled into past emotions she thought she buried.

The heart has memory. You can forgive a man intellectually and still hurt emotionally. You can move on physically and still be tied spiritually. You can stop speaking to him and still speak to him in your reactions. The heart has a memory. And memory is not healed by time—it is healed by truth, revelation, and the Holy Spirit. Until that healing happens, the mother-child relationship will be influenced by something deeper: the residue of what the father left behind.

And because children are present, innocent, and emotionally open, they sometimes absorb the emotional charge that wasn't meant for them. Not the blame. Not the responsibility. Just the emotional weight.

The child becomes the "safe place" for unresolved pain. Women often hold themselves together in public. They hold themselves together at work. They hold themselves together around friends. But home is where the heart exhales. Home is where the internal world becomes visible. Home is the only place where a woman feels safe enough to feel everything.

So, the child gets the unfiltered version of her emotional state, her stress, her sadness, her resentment, her fear, her anger, her anxiety. Not because she doesn't love the child, but because she has nowhere else to put it.

The father is gone. He is, for any reason, unavailable, unreachable, or emotionally distant. He is not there to receive the disappointment he created. So, the emotions fall downward— toward the child who is present, available, and tender. This is not a mother's fault. This is the natural flow of unhealed wounds.

But the Holy Spirit can reroute the flow. He can pull the emotions back to their rightful target— not to harm the man, but to free the woman. The Holy Spirit is our Comforter, Deliverer, and Healer.

Until she is free from negative emotional ties to him, and to the memory of the loss, disappointment, hurt, or abandonment, she cannot be fully free to love the child without interference.

> But the Comforter, which is the Holy Ghost, whom the Father will send in my name, he shall teach you all things, and bring all things to your remembrance, whatsoever I have said unto you. (John 14:26)

This chapter, this book is not about blame; it is about awareness—mostly self-awareness. Because once a woman understands *why* she reacts, *where* the emotion comes from, *how* the father still influences her heart, and *why* certain behaviors trigger her— she can finally separate the strands. She can say "This emotion is not about my child. This is about the man. This is about my heart.

This is about what I survived." That clarity alone begins healing. It breaks confusion. It breaks guilt. It breaks shame. It breaks false narratives about the mother. And it gives her room to breathe, think clearly, and love fully.

That invisible emotional pain tie can be broken.

Not by the child. Not by the man. Not by time. Not by pretending it doesn't exist. But by the Holy Spirit, who specializes in severing emotional cords that were never meant to govern a woman's future.

This chapter prepares the mother for that breaking— not to disconnect from the child, but to disconnect the child from the shadows of the father.

To finally love the child as God intended: cleanly, wholly, freely, and without the weight of another person's sins.

CHAPTER 3

The Child Who Becomes the Reminder

When the Heart Responds to the Father, Not the Child

There are mothers who look at their child and feel a sudden wave of emotion they cannot explain. Sometimes it is sadness. Sometimes anger. Sometimes frustration. Sometimes heaviness. Sometimes fear. Sometimes anxiety. Sometimes resentment. Sometimes exhaustion far deeper than the day's events justify.

Most women blame themselves for these reactions. They think, "Why am I feeling this?" "What's wrong with me?" "I love my child. Why does my heart feel conflicted?" "Why do I feel overwhelmed when they walk into the room?" "Why am I irritated, and I don't know why?" The answer is seldom about the child. It is almost always about the **reminder.**

Children carry the echo of the man—even when the mother doesn't want them to. A child can become a living reminder of the relationship that failed, the promises that were broken, the betrayal that wounded, the abandonment that scarred, the season of life the mother barely survived, the man who never grew up, the man who lied, manipulated, or disappointed, the dreams she

16

once had that never materialized, the version of herself she no longer wants to remember. Because of this, every time the child laughs, frowns, misbehaves, grows, asks questions, needs attention, or simply looks like the father, the mother feels something resurface inside her — not because she dislikes the child, but because the child awakens emotions that were never healed.

The child does not know this. The mother may not fully understand it. She may not be aware of it. She may be aware, but think she is hiding it. She can't—if it is not on her face, it will find her voice, if her voice denies to speak it, it will flow into to the environment and it may be in audible and invisible, but it is there. The household feels the tension but either cannot name it. It could be that it is so big and horrible that everyone refuses to name it. To a little child it could be, "Mommy is mad at me."

This is how generational patterns stay alive: in silence, in confusion, in unnamed wounds.

The trigger has a shape. Children trigger mothers in different ways, especially when the father-wound is active. A mother may see his facial expression. A look the child gives feels familiar — too familiar.

His personality - Stubbornness, sensitivity, humor, silence, moodiness.

His emotional traits - How the child withdraws, engages, reacts, or communicates.

His failures - The child's struggles feel like the father's mistakes repeating.

His absence - The child exists, but the man is gone — and the heart resents the imbalance.

His season of life - The moment the child reaches the age when the relationship fell apart.

His DNA - The undeniable genetic imprint that ties the child to the man.

And this is almost inevitable, when the child can communicate, they start to query the mother about their daddy. "Where is he?" "Is he coming back?" "When is he coming back?" When the child begins to romanticize the father, "I wish daddy was here." If mother isn't healed by then, a near-war may be their everyday household scenario. She is thinking, 'That creep; child, if only you knew.' In her desire not to turn the child against their father she may say nothing negative about the father, or try to say something neutral because she loves her child and doesn't want to deepen the hurt.

The child may have already taken this to the level of "If it weren't for you, Daddy would be here." "If it weren't for you, Dady wouldn't have left." "You're mean, you ran Daddy off."

None of this is the child's fault. None of it is chosen. But the heart reacts anyway. A child is supposed to have a father and a mother. But by this time the wound is fresh every day and now the child keeps picking the scab off--, even if it is a pseudo-scab, where the mother is trying everything she knows to heal or at least stop the hurt. The emotional memory of the father remains in the mother's body, soul, and nervous system and keeps wounding, day after day. It does not mean that she wants that man back, she just didn't like the nuclear fallout of his actions, words, lies, unavailability, unsupportive nature, and disappearance.

The emotional misfire can occur when a child triggers an old memory, the mother's heart may snap, shut down, become impatient, become defensive, become overwhelmed, withdraw emotionally, overreact to small issues, feel resentment she doesn't understand, feel pressure that doesn't match the moment. She may parent from fear instead of Wisdom, or parent from memory instead of truth. This is not intentional. This is trauma speaking.

The mother's unhealed trauma has either all at once, or slowly over time, traumatized the child. Trauma results can be contagious, and the house is an emotional hospital with two people in the same hospital room. What did you think would happen? Momma is pretending to be okay or even strong, and while not always right, kids are very perceptive. What do you think would happen?

Trauma is not always catastrophic events. Trauma is anything the heart never fully processed. Pain that was never spoken becomes pain that speaks through reactions.

The child interprets it incorrectly. Children interpret emotional distance as, "I'm not good enough." "She doesn't want me." "Something is wrong with me." "I'm a burden." "I make mommy unhappy." "I'm the problem."

They have no idea they triggered a memory—not a judgment. A wound—not a rejection. A reminder—not a resentment. They only feel the emotional climate and assume responsibility.

This is how generational wounds pass to the next branch of the family tree. Not through abuse. Not through violence. But through silence, confusion, and misinterpretation.

The mother interprets it incorrectly too. She may think, "I'm failing." "Something is wrong with me." "I'm not maternal enough." "I'm too damaged to be a good mother." "Maybe my child deserves better." "Why can't I bond the way I want to?" These are lies that embarrassment whispers into her heart.

Motherhood is not failing. Her heart is grieving. She is not rejecting her child. She is reacting to her past instead of living in her present. These confusing feelings are not a sign she is unfit— they are signs she is wounded. And every wound can heal.

Every pattern can break. Every reminder can lose its power. God does not leave mothers with unprocessed pain. One of the most tender things about God is this: **He refuses to let a woman's past govern the destiny of her**

child; but you must agree with God. Let the healing flow.

He exposes patterns gently. He unravels emotional knots slowly. He brings awareness without shame. He reveals without condemning. He heals without humiliating. He knows that if the mother heals, the child heals automatically. Because motherhood is generational architecture. And when the architect is restored, the house becomes safe again.

A child's purpose is separate from the father's failure. Every child from a broken relationship carries two parallel histories: the history of the parents, and the destiny God designed. These two things are not equal.

The destiny is always greater. But the destiny becomes clearer when the mother heals the emotional connection between the child and the memory of the father.

Let this chapter is the doorway to that healing. Let it be the moment where the mother can say, "This reaction is not about my child. This reaction is about what I survived." "And I don't have to live like this anymore." "And my child will not inherit what hurt me."

The reminder only has power when the wound is still open. God is ready to close it.

CHAPTER 4

The Echo of Abandonment

How Father-Wounds Shape Motherhood Even When a
Woman Thinks She's "Fine"

Abandonment leaves a sound in the soul. Not a scream, not a cry or a shout. But an echo, perhaps a still quiet voice that is not God, but pain persistently vibrating, affecting everything near to it.

Women often pride themselves on survival; they have to. They pick up the pieces. They adjust. They figure it out. They carry the home, the job, the bills, the emotions, the responsibilities, and the future — all at once. The must sometimes rebuild where they never expected the building to have failed.

When a man leaves — physically, emotionally, spiritually, financially, or mentally — a woman often steps into strength so quickly that she doesn't realize the wound is still open. The woman has the helper anointing, and that means she can most often multitask and do a number of things. She is the helpmeet, but when there is no husband, it is as though she's offering adjectives where there is no noun. It works for a while, but not as it should, as she hopes, or as God designed.

And the Lord God said, It is not good that the man should be alone; I will make him an help meet for him.
(Genesis 2:18)

Question*: If it is not good for man to be alone, then why would it be good for a woman?*

She thinks "I moved on." "I'm over him." "I'm not bothered anymore." "I'm focused on my child." "I'm fine." But the heart can say "I'm fine" long before it's healed. Abandonment does not announce itself. It hides in the corners of the soul. And those corners become the places where motherhood begins to echo.

Abandonment changes the atmosphere inside a woman. When a man leaves, something shifts inside a woman's emotional world. Part of her becomes hyper-independent, part of her becomes protective, part of her becomes guarded, part of her becomes exhausted, part of her becomes defensive, part of her becomes numb, part of her becomes over-responsible, part of her becomes fearful of being disappointed again.

These parts don't disappear when she gives birth. They simply fold into motherhood. She may not call it abandonment, she may call it strength, or survival, or "doing what I had to do." But the echo remains.

It whispers when she's tired. It rises when she feels unsupported. It speaks when she sees the father's absence reflected in her child's needs.

Women must realize that abandonment speaks. It says things like, "You're doing this alone." "No one is coming to help." "You have to be everything." "Don't trust anyone." "You can't relax." "You can't be vulnerable." "Don't let the child get too close; closeness invites pain." "Don't show weakness." "Don't depend on anyone." The voice of abandonment is missed because of the sheer love he feels for her child. She can go into momma-bear mode and become fierce. And, or she can take on the spirit of a man, which she was never designed to carry be in. Distortions start, but she may never see them because she is 'doing what she has to do.'

The most dangerous whisper: "Your child might hurt you the way he did." This may sound like, "Does everyone leave me?" This whisper is not logical. It is not based in truth. It is a fear echo — the residue of emotional abandonment that spills into motherhood. If the child and the mother are feeling this or listening to this whisper, what do you think will happen in that house—over time?

This fear is rarely conscious, but it shapes how a woman protects her heart. Some protect by withdrawing. Some protect by controlling. Some protect by numbing. Some protect by staying angry. Some protect by overparenting. Some protect by under-parenting. Some protect by shutting down the softer parts of themselves, or as said, taking on new personas that God never intended for a woman. The child does not cause this. The father-wound does.

The nervous system remembers abandonment. Even when the mind moves on, the body remembers. A mother may experience sudden irritation, overwhelm, emotional shutdown, anxiety, fear of being needed, fear of being loved, fear of being hurt, hypervigilance, an inability to rest, or guilt when she feels disconnected. She may feel stress when the child shows emotion, or confusion, she may react more strongly than the situation requires. These are signs that her nervous system is still responding or re-reacting to the father's abandonment, not the child's presence.

The real issue is this abandonment, and all the overwhelming responsibilities have thrown her into survival mode. Unless God heals this, it will only get worse from here. By not choice or plan of his own, the child simply turns the volume up on what was already inside her.

This abandonment distorts the view of the child. 'Even though he's gone, my life could go back to normal if I didn't have you,' is what she may think. Dear God, do not let her say that to her child, although too many mothers may have. A mother may unconsciously project the wounds of the father onto the child when she fears the child will also leave her. She may fear that the child will disappoint her, or feel angry because the child still needs her when she has nothing left. Feelings of resentment may rise because she is alone in the parenting, feels guilt for being overloaded and overwhelmed. She feels afraid of loving too deeply, feels punished by the father's absence, feels pressured by the demands of parenting without support, feels triggered just because the child may resemble the father—or even if the child looks nothing like the father. This is her tether she may think.

She may not identify it as abandonment trauma. She may call it exhaustion, or impatience, or worry about how to pay all these bills. She may think this is "just how life is." But the root is deeper.

The echo is louder than the event, especially if she rehearses it, even mentally, silently. The echo keeps repeating so by its repetition it keeps the pain alive. The echo does not mean the mother is broken, it means she loved deeply. Only deep love creates deep wounds. Only deep wounds create deep echoes. A woman who felt nothing would have recovered instantly. A woman who loved nothing would not have cared. A woman with no emotional investment would have walked away without a scar.

Women who carry abandonment wounds carry them because they gave their heart away—fully, sincerely, and often sacrificially. Motherhood does not erase that wound. It reveals it because it is a different kind of love. And God's intention is not to shame the woman for the wound, but to **heal** it.

God heals the echo before he heals the behavior. Most mothers focus on their reactions: "I shouldn't have snapped." "I shouldn't have withdrawn." "I should be more patient." "I should be more affectionate." "I should be stronger." But God doesn't start with behavior. He starts with wounds. He heals, abandonment, betrayal,

26

disappointment, emotional abandonment, rejection, broken promises, the fear of being alone, the fear of repeating patterns, the fear of loving and losing again.

When the echo is healed, the reactions disappear naturally. This is why this chapter matters. A woman cannot fix reactions until she heals the original injury— the core wound.

Healing starts with recognition. A mother can begin healing the echo of abandonment by saying, "This feeling is not about my child. This is about the father. This is about what I survived. This is the wound speaking, not my heart." This single moment of clarity breaks years of confusion because the moment a woman separates the child from the wound; the echo loses power. Her love becomes clearer. Her responses become softer. Her heart becomes lighter. And the child begins to feel the difference immediately. Because when a woman heals, the whole house heals with her.

CHAPTER 5

Emotional Substitution

When the Child Carries the Emotional Weight Meant for the Father

One of the most misunderstood dynamics in motherhood is emotional substitution, which is the silent, unintentional transfer of emotional weight from the father to the child. It happens quietly. It happens invisibly, without intention or awareness. But when a woman has nowhere to place the weight of her disappointment, grief, heartbreak, betrayal, or abandonment… the child becomes the emotional stand-in. Not because the mother wants that or is choosing it. It is not because she lacks love, but because her heart needs somewhere safe to release the pressure. And the child — present, innocent, close, and emotionally open — becomes the place where that pressure lands.

But she loves her child so much. Yes, imagine her agony, torn in those two directions at once.

What is emotional substitution? Emotional substitution happens when a mother reacts to the child with emotions meant for the father. This substitution carries resentment toward the child without knowing why. It is as though she expects the child to "make up" for the father. She feels disappointment the child never caused, feels frustration that belongs to past events, holds the child to standards shaped by the father's failure. Mom may become triggered by the child's behaviors that resemble the father. She may feel abandoned—then expresses that feeling toward the child. She may feel betrayed—then becomes guarded with the child. She may feel unloved by the father—then questions the child's affection, feels unprotected—then becomes controlling, feels unsupported—then becomes resentful, feels used or taken advantage of—then becomes defensive. It is a serious cascade.

In simple terms the child becomes the emotional outlet for an adult wound. Not intentionally. Not maliciously. Not consciously. It is automatic, quiet, and rooted in pain the mother never had a chance to verbalize.

Why does this happen?

Because the heart cannot hold unresolved emotions forever. When the father is absent, unavailable, unwilling, unsafe, uninterested, disengaged, inconsistent, or emotionally immature, the mother often has no partner to express her feelings to. So, the emotions remain stored inside her. But stored pain always seeks expression. And since the father is gone— either emotionally or physically, the emotions shift toward the place where the relational energy is still active: **the child.** The child did not cause the heartache. The child only carries the proximity. And proximity absorbs pressure.

The substitution shows up in subtle ways. Many mothers don't see it because it appears in soft, ordinary moments. Irritation at normal childlike behavior. But the irritation is heavier than the moment requires. Impatience doesn't match the situation. Her reaction is really for the father, not the child. Feeling overwhelmed by the child's need for attention because the emotional tank was drained by the father long before motherhood began.

• **Resentment for having to carry everything alone - this is emotional, not logical.** the child is not the one who left — the father is.

• **Sadness when the child resembles the father -** The resemblance reawakens the wound.

• **Distance when the child gets older -** Because older children resemble the man even more, and they are probably about to leave her.

• **Overparenting or under-parenting -** Trying to compensate, or trying not to feel.

• **Emotional fatigue that shows up as withdrawal -** The mother is not tired of the child — she is tired of the father's absence.

Emotional substitution is not abuse. Nor is it intentional harm. It is the evidence of a heart trying to survive unresolved pain.

A child does not know he or she is carrying emotions that don't belong to them. They assume, "Mom is upset at me." "I'm doing something wrong." "I'm too much." "I make Mommy sad." "My existence is a burden." "I remind her of something bad." "Maybe she doesn't like me." (Heck a lot of adults have inner children who still behave that way.)

They do not know they are holding emotional weight meant for a grown tail man. And when a child carries weight that isn't theirs, they grow up with questions they never deserved.

Emotional substitution affects the mother by creating inner conflict. She loves the child deeply. She feels guilty for reactions she can't explain. She feels ashamed for emotions that confuse her. She feels overwhelmed and doesn't know why. She feels judged by others. She feels like she's "failing" even when she isn't.

But the truth is simple and liberating, **She is not failing. She is hurting. And hurt tries to find a place to land.**

God never intended for a child to carry an adult's pain. The child is meant to carry purpose, not punishment. The child carries destiny, not disappointment. The child carries identity, not past memory. The child is a blessing, not a substitute. The child is a gift, not a reminder. God sees the emotional transfer. He hears the silent cries. He understands the weight. And He gently calls the mother to healing, not because she is wrong, but because she has carried more than she was ever designed to carry.

The first step of healing: returning the weight to God – unless God is the *Daddy* that you are mad at. The emotional weight meant for the father cannot be given to anyone else. Not to the child, to friends, not really to another man. Not to extended family, not even to the father himself. Only God can hold it. Only God can untangle it. Only God can absorb it. Only God can transform it. Only God can remove its power.

When a woman begins to give the weight back to God, the child becomes free — instantly, spiritually, emotionally, atmospherically. Because God takes what the child should never have been carrying. Healing begins when the mother realizes "This emotion isn't about my child. This is about himself. And I don't have to carry this anymore. I can let God take it."

This moment breaks generational inheritance. This moment resets the emotional temperature of the home. This moment releases mother and child from misunderstanding. And this moment marks the beginning of deep, generational healing.

CHAPTER 6

Who *You* Mad At?

When the __Daddy__ You're Mad At… Is God!

Many exhausted, overwhelmed people – even mothers are secretly angry at God. When your father and other forsake you, the Lord will take you up. Many may be wondering, why hasn't God taken me up? Is God really there? Then shouldn't He be helping me? Too many folks are mad at God because they think God is a vending machine who should just supply everything they need or want when they want it.

> For ye have not received the spirit of bondage again to fear; but ye have received the Spirit of adoption, whereby we cry, Abba, Father. (Romans 8:15)

Well, folks let's see if God can help us after we've gotten ourselves into some stuff. Did we acknowledge God through the process of this dating, marriage—if no marriage the choice to have sex outside of marriage and then become pregnant? Don't worry, God will not hold anything against you, but you must come to Him truthfully and repent. Now God can help you. God is not holding anything against women and especially not against children or if you've become poor or feel poor for taking care of all the expenses yourself, God has a real heart toward you.

But I'll address how you may be feeling, not because you're rebellious, disrespectful or disobedient. Not because of unbelief, but from disappointment, when you've had to lower your expectations down to nothing. It comes from exhaustion, betrayal by earthly fathers, abandonment by men, unfair responsibility, chronic overwhelm, unanswered prayers, carrying burdens alone, doing dual parenting without dual support.

Women are NOT mad at God as GOD. They're mad at the **Father-role** they *needed* God to fill—even though they may have found an earthly, inappropriate substitute that didn't work out. This is important.

Scripture is full of people mad at God. Job, David ("How long, O Lord?"), Naomi ("The Almighty has dealt bitterly with me"), Jeremiah ("You deceived me, Lord"), Moses ("Why have You afflicted Your servant?"). This shows moms they are *human.* And it shows that they can talk to God.

Women often unconsciously project their earthly father's failures, their husband's failures, abandonment, neglect, emotional distance, silence …onto God. So, the anger is not really "theology" — it's trauma wearing spiritual clothing.

When we've done it our way and turned our back on God, how can we blame God for not being there? If we've not repented, if we have not invited God back into our lives and daily choices and actions, God may just not be there, except by His Mercy. In your repentance, be sure to repent of idolatry if you over admired the person, the human being that you thought would be your everything from kinsman redeemer, to provider, healer, and the giver of all joy. And they just left. Trust this: If you idolized them, then they had to leave. And that would be because of God's great Mercy – so He wouldn't have to judge either of you for idolatry.

God is not the father who left, God is not the father who ignored. God is not the father who yelled. God is not the father who paid no child support. God is not the father who never showed up. God is not the father who broke promises.

"Your anger is not an enemy of God. Talk to God, He can handle whatever you have to say. Your silence is the enemy of your healing. Unless your silence is you listening to God to hear what He has to say to you, by His Holy Spirit.

God wants you to come to Him. He wants to hear you, help you, and heal you. He will invite and he will deal with you gently and without condemnation. Psalm after psalm shows God responding to anger with **comfort**, not punishment.

God is not offended by a mother's exhaustion. He is not surprised by her tears. He is not pushed away by her frustration. He is the one Father who actually stays.

If you have felt abandoned, prayed with no answers, carried motherhood alone, lost trust in men, lost trust in fatherhood itself, then look for God.

Come near to God and he will come near to you. Wash your hands, you sinners, and purify your hearts, you double-minded. (James 4:8))

CHAPTER 7

The Spiritual Cost of Bitterness

How Bitterness Transfers Through Generations Without Intention

Bitterness does not begin loud; it begins quietly—, in disappointment, in betrayal, in heartbreak, in abandonment, in dreams that never materialized, in memories that never closed, in words that were never spoken, in apologies that never came. Naomi said that God had dealt bitterly with her. Naomi lost her husband, and her sons so she had no men in her life. Isn't that a spawn of bitterness to lose the man or men in your life? Bitterness starts as a wound. But unhealed wounds become roots. And roots grow, even when we are not looking.

Many women do not realize they are bitter. They think they are strong, focused, independent, responsible, guarded, resilient, "just tired, " "just doing it on my own," And they think they deserve to *feel* this way.

But bitterness is not always obvious. It is almost never emotional. It is almost always spiritual. Bitterness is the spiritual scar tissue around a heart that was not protected, not honored, and not valued--, not even understood by the man who fathered her child. Yoo many people, even men don't have a handle on their own emotions so they have no empathy or ability to help you with yours.

Bitterness—however small or justified—has a spiritual cost.

Bitterness is not anger — it is injury that hardened; it is unforgiveness *morphed*. Anger is the flame. Bitterness is the ash. Anger comes and goes. Bitterness stays and settles. Anger reacts. Bitterness remembers. Anger explodes. Unforgiveness festers into bitterness that erodes.

Bitterness is not loud. Bitter women often never raise their voice. Many are sweet, responsible, loving, hardworking, and deeply sacrificial. Bitterness is not loud — it is *heavy*. It's heavy on the heart, heavy on the home, heavy on the atmosphere, and heavy on the mother-child dynamic.

Bitterness comes with a spirit – that means it is anointed, by the dark kingdom.

Bitterness is more than an emotion. It is a spiritual weight that affects everything around it. Scripture warns about bitterness because defiles many (Hebrews 12:15). It poisons environments and contaminates relationships. It masks itself as strength, but is not. Bitterness limits the ability to trust and drains joy. It changes people; it reshapes personality and alters perception. Worse of all, bitterness transfers—directly, spiritually, and silently—into the next generation.

Children breathe bitterness the same way they breathe air from the home. They feel it in tension. They feel it in tone. They feel it in silence. They feel it in the emotional weather of the home. Even if the mother never speaks a negative word.

Bitterness can appear subtly in a mother's behavior shortening her patience, closing her heart, making her quick to withdraw, and slow to forgive. It gives her a giving her a defensive posture, making her feel unsafe emotionally, and overprotective. Bitterness makes her judgmental toward the child's choices and makes her assume motives. She is unable to rest. She is and feels unsupported even when help is offered.

Most heartbreaking of all, bitterness makes a woman slow to receive love from her own child. Not because she doesn't want love, but because bitterness hardened the places where affection should land. So the child grows up feeling "Mom doesn't like me." "Mom is disappointed in me." "Mom doesn't trust me." "Mom doesn't soften toward me." "Mom is always tense around me."

But the truth is: The mother is not angry at the child. She is unhealed from the father.

Bitterness transfers when it is unnamed. Bitterness does not need to be spoken to be transferred. It transfers through emotional stiffness, harsh tone, guardedness, perfectionism, lack of affection, chronic frustration, heaviness in the atmosphere, reluctance to celebrate, difficulty expressing joy, distance when the child needs closeness, tension the child cannot explain. Children grow up in the echo of their mother's mood. If bitterness shapes her mood, it shapes their emotional blueprint. They learn to guard, to detach and to silence their needs. They to overperform and learn to expect disappointment or to assume abandonment. They learn to be cautious with love, to carry responsibility that isn't theirs.

Bitterness has a root and it takes up residence in families and bloodlines.

This is how generational cycles begin--Not through dysfunction, but through unspoken, unhealed wounds.

Bitterness blocks the mother's capacity to receive from God. This is one of the greatest spiritual costs. A bitter heart struggles to receive comfort, encouragement, reassurance, affection, softness, spiritual intimacy, peace, joy, hope. Not because God is absent— but because bitterness numbs the heart's receptors.

When a mother cannot receive from God, she cannot pour into the child in the way she desires. Her spiritual inheritance becomes limited. Her emotional availability becomes restricted. Her joy gets capped. Her ability to trust gets minimized. And the child, who needs a spiritually open mother, feels the effect long before they can name it.

God has extreme compassion for bitter women. A bitter woman is a wounded woman. A woman whose heart was stretched too far. A woman who trusted someone who let her fall. A woman who carried more than one heart can carry. A woman who had to be stronger than she wanted to be. A woman who cried silently because there was no one safe to talk to. A woman who lost dreams and had to keep functioning anyway. God does not condemn bitter women— He **rescues** them.

He restores their softness. He melts the hardness. He washes away the residue. He brings them back to emotional life. Bitterness is not a moral failure. It is a spiritual infection that God knows how to heal fully and permanently.

Healing begins when bitterness is named. When a woman says, "I'm hurting more than I realized." "I never healed from what he did." "This pain is still shaping me." "I'm tired of carrying this." "I don't want to pass this to my child." that is the moment bitterness begins to die. Because bitterness cannot survive exposure. Bitterness thrives in secrecy. Bitterness grows in silence. Bitterness strengthens in denial.

But the moment a woman names the wound, God releases grace into that place. Grace softens. Grace loosens roots. Grace pulls out poison. Grace restores tenderness. Grace returns joy. Grace rewrites legacy.

Breaking the Cycle Saves the Next Generation. A healed mother creates a healed home. A healed home births healed children. Healed children become healed adults. Healed adults raise healed families.

One woman's healing becomes a generational turning point. God never intended bitterness to govern motherhood. He intended motherhood to be a place of love, joy, connection, and spiritual abundance. When bitterness is uprooted, the atmosphere changes. The mother changes. The child changes. The whole family line changes. And that is the spiritual miracle God wants to perform.

CHAPTER 8

Open Doors

How Pain Becomes a Pattern

Pain does not stay still. Pain moves. Pain spreads. Pain opens spiritual and emotional doors the same way a draft moves through a house with cracks in the walls. And if the pain is not identified, healed, or surrendered to God, it slowly becomes a **pattern**—a repeating emotional cycle that affects every room of a mother's life and every corner of her child's heart.

Patterns look normal because they become familiar. But familiarity doesn't mean healthy. And repeated doesn't mean right. Patterns form when pain goes unaddressed long enough to become a rhythm.

A mother does not choose the pattern. The pattern selects and seeks her out, even choosing her wounds.

A wound becomes a gateway. A wound becomes a pattern when the heart doesn't have a safe place to heal, emotions get buried instead of processed, bitterness isn't recognized, abandonment never gets acknowledged, loneliness becomes a lifestyle, stress becomes routine, heartbreak becomes part of her identity, the father's absence becomes normal, survival replaces emotional rest,

43

At first the wound is a moment. Then it becomes a season. Then it becomes a habit. Then it becomes a personality trait that isn't actually her personality at all. The open door is often small— just a crack, just a space, just a gap. But through that gap, emotional patterns slip through until the mother is responding to life not from her present reality, but from yesterday's injury.

Pain repeats until it's healed. Emotional patterns do not form because a woman is weak. They form because the wound still demands attention. A wounded heart repeats itself until it gets relief. That repetition may look like:

• **Recurring frustration** - Every little thing feels bigger than it should.

• **Emotional exhaustion** - The mother can't understand why she's tired after doing "nothing dramatic."

• **Cycles of resentment** - Not at the child — but at the situation.

• **Overreaction to small issues** - The "small issue" triggered a large internal memory.

• **Distance in connection** - The mother pulls away, not because she doesn't love the child, but because the open door drains her emotional energy.

• **Repeating the same arguments** - The pattern speaks louder than logic.

• Feeling triggered by the child's resemblance to the father

The resemblance activates the wound. These are not failures. These are signals. Signals that pain is asking to be healed.

Patterns often begin in self-protection. When a mother is hurt, her spirit often says "I will never feel that pain again." That vow may look like emotional withdrawal, heightened vigilance, controlling behaviors, perfectionism, shutting down, keeping the child at emotional arm's length, avoiding deep conversations, becoming overly strict, becoming overly lenient, avoiding vulnerability, staying busy to avoid feeling. Not relying on anyone, expecting disappointment.

These are not sins—these are coping mechanisms. But coping is not healing. Coping is surviving. And survival is not the abundant life God promised.

Unhealed pain becomes the parent. If the wound is not healed, the wound becomes the "third parent" in the home. The mother does not want this. The child does not understand it. Yet the wound shapes the mother's tone, the atmosphere of the home, the level of affection, the emotional boundaries, the connection between mother and child, the way love is expressed, the comfort available when the child is hurting, the spiritual climate of the family. The wound begins to do the talking, the reacting, the correcting, the disciplining, the withdrawing, even the loving.

Not because the mother wants this— but because the wound hasn't been closed.

Children carry what their mothers don't heal. This is why open doors matter. Children absorb: the atmosphere, the unspoken tensions, the emotional climate, the fears, the frustration, the anxiety, the bitterness, the abandonment echoes, the patterns the mother didn't choose but lived through. The child doesn't just inherit the father's DNA, but also the father's mistakes. That is nature and it is the subject of another book.

The child also inherits the emotional environment shaped by the wound; that is nurture. And they grow up forming their own patterns from that space. This is how generational cycles start without anyone doing anything "wrong." The cycle isn't intentional. It's inherited and it is environmental.

God always shuts doors He didn't open. The enemy uses trauma and pain as a doorway. God uses healing as a lock. Healing doesn't erase history — it closes the spiritual and emotional doors that history opened. God closes doors when a woman becomes aware, she names the pattern, and she begins to talk to God about it. God heals when she confronts the root (not just the symptoms), she forgives the father, she releases bitterness, she stops carrying emotional weight meant for someone else, she invites God into the part of her heart she tried to protect, she allows herself to feel again, she lets go of defensiveness, she breaks inner vows. And when the door closes, the pattern breaks.

Not gradually— but spiritually, immediately. The emotional atmosphere clears. The child feels a difference even if they can't articulate it. The home becomes lighter. The mother feels like herself again. The generational cycle loses its power. God specializes in closing doors that pain opened--, healing trauma.

Awareness is the first step, not the last. If you found yourself in this chapter saying, "This is me." "I see the pattern." "I feel the open door." "I didn't know why this kept happening." Awareness is not condemnation. Awareness is deliverance.

The moment a woman sees the pattern, the pattern has already started to break. Awareness brings choice. Choice brings healing. Healing brings restoration, the kind that rewrites the family's story.

CHAPTER 9

When Resentment Becomes a Lens

How Motherhood Becomes Reactive Instead of Nurturing

Resentment doesn't always look like anger. Sometimes it looks like exhaustion, irritability, emotional fatigue, emotional distance, numbness, sharpness in tone, impatience, tension, heaviness, and frustration that "doesn't make sense", shutting down, losing joy, feeling overwhelmed by normal tasks.

Most mothers experiencing resentment do not feel hatred. They feel **pressure**. Pressure that was caused by the father's absence, not the child's presence. But resentment doesn't know how to aim itself correctly. So it becomes a *lens* a filter over the mother's emotional world.

Through that filter, she experiences the child differently: small behaviors feel bigger. Innocent questions feel exhausting. Normal needs feel demanding. Expressions of love feel overwhelming. The child's personality feels irritating. Teaching moments feel draining, affection feels costly, discipline feels too heavy Connection feels complicated, The mother often feels guilty, confused, or ashamed. She begins not to even recognize herself. She wonders where her softness went. She feels like her reactions don't match her heart.

Because they don't.

She isn't reacting to the child. She's reacting through the lens of resentment.

Resentment is a work of the flesh; it is a distortion, not a character flaw. Resentment does not reflect a woman's heart; it reflects a woman's wound. When the lens is resentment, the heart sees everything through the shadow of abandonment, betrayal, disappointment, broken promises, emotional abandonment, injustice, isolation, and lack of support. The mother is not hard-hearted. She is heart-hurt.

Resentment distorts perception in subtle ways:

• **It magnifies minor issues** - What should be a 1 becomes a 5.

• **It interprets normal needs as burdens** - Not because the child is a burden, but because the mother's heart is burdened.

• **It makes the mother feel alone even in moments of connection.** The residue of abandonment echoes louder than present reality.

• **It makes joy harder to access.** The emotional channel is blocked.

• **It makes the child feel like "too much."** Because the mother's heart is operating with a deficit.

None of this is intentional; and all of it is painful. Resentment is the emotional smoke from a fire the father lit.

Resentment begins when expectations were shattered, promises were broken, the father left emotionally or physically, the mother had to carry double loads, the child became a reminder of pain, survival replaced support, exhaustion replaced partnership, protection replaced affection. Resentment forms because the mother gave more than she had, for longer than she should have, with less support than she deserved.

Resentment is not a choice, entirely. It is a work of the flesh and we should resist such, but it it easier said than done. There is an evil anointing to all flesh works that tempt humans to embrace them as if it will help them help them or as if they deserve to misbehave in this way. It is a *symptom*. And the presence of resentment does not mean the mother is unloving— it means she is overextended.

Resentment affects how the mother interprets the child. When a resentment lens forms, the child may be interpreted as demanding, needy, difficult, too sensitive, too emotional, too much like the father, too easily triggered, resistant, disrespectful, or stubborn.

But these interpretations often have nothing to do with the child and everything to do with the emotional frame the mother is viewing from.

A child asking for help is not "demanding." A child crying is not "too sensitive." A child needing reassurance is not "draining." A child expressing emotion is not "being dramatic." A child making mistakes is not "disrespectful." A child needing guidance is not "difficult." Resentment distorts reality.

The mother is not seeing the child — she is seeing the *echo of the father*.

Until the lens is healed.

The child responds to the lens, not the tone. Children have sensitive spirits; they can feel the lens before the words:

- They sense tension.

- They sense withdrawal.

- They sense disappointment that isn't theirs.

- They sense frustration that isn't fair.

- They sense distance even when the mother is present.

Children respond to the emotional climate, not the explanation. So, they adapt or they try to. They shrink. They harden. They overperform. They become anxious. They learn to walk on eggshells. They try to "fix" things they didn't break. All because the lens of resentment has colored the atmosphere.

51

Resentment makes motherhood feel like a weight instead of a joy. When resentment is active, motherhood starts to feel like a responsibility instead of a relationship. It feels like a a duty instead of a delight, a burden instead of a blessing. This flows into survival mode now; it feels like survival instead of connection

The mother often feels guilty because she loves her child deeply — yet feels drained in ways that don't match the child's behavior. Because the exhaustion isn't from the child. It's from the wound.

Resentment is a sign the heart needs rest. It is a sign that the resentful heart needs correction, not a sign the child needs correction.

God Heals the Lens Before He Heals the Interactions. A mother often tries to fix her behavior by saying, "I'm going to be more patient." "I'm going to stop snapping." "I'm going to soften my tone." "I'm going to be more affectionate." "I'm going to react differently next time." These efforts can be sincere, but they are temporary because behavior follows perspective, and perspective comes from the lens.

God does not begin with behavior, He begins with vision.

He heals the lens so the mother can clearly see the child as separate from the father. She can then see the child's innocence and true personality. She sees her child's needs without undue exhaustion. She sees herself with compassion. She looks on her own pain with truth and her home with spiritual clarity.

Once the lens heals, the behavior naturally shifts because the heart finally sees the child correctly.

When the Lens Breaks, the Bond Restores. The moment resentment lifts — the home changes. The air feels lighter. The child becomes calmer. Affection becomes easier. Connection becomes sweeter. Patience becomes natural. Motherhood feels like breathing again. The mother's heart softens. The child feels safe. The atmosphere becomes peaceful. The emotional climate resets.

Resentment was never the mother's personality. It was the pain speaking. And when pain loses its voice, love becomes the loudest sound in the home.

CHAPTER 10

Breaking Shame Off Women

Why Mothers Aren't "Bad"—They're Wounded

Shame is the heaviest emotion a woman can carry. It is heavier than guilt, regret, sadness, or grief. Shame whispers, "You're the problem." "You're failing." "You're a bad mother." "You're hurting your child." "You're too emotional." "You're not emotional enough." "You're damaged." "You can't fix this." "You're ruining everything." "You should be better than this by now." But shame never tells the truth.

The truth is simple: **Women do not act out of wickedness; they act out of wounds.** There is no such thing as a "bad mother." Only wounded mothers. Overwhelmed mothers. Exhausted mothers. Unsupported mothers. Heartbroken mothers. Mothers who were left to carry what two adults created. Mothers who never had a safe place to fall apart. Mothers who gave more love than they received. Mothers who were asked to be strong when they were still bleeding inside.

Shame blinds women to their own goodness. Healing reveals it.

Shame forms when pain has nowhere to go. Most women do not talk about their pain. They hide it because they don't want to be judged, they don't want their child to feel responsible. They don't want to seem weak. They don't want to look like they're failing. They don't want others to know how much the father hurt them. They don't want pity. They don't want to be misunderstood. They don't have anyone safe to talk to, so, the pain stays inside. And whatever stays inside too is something that tries to hide, or the person tries to hide it because it has become their shame.

Shame is unspoken grief. Shame is hidden sorrow. Shame is buried disappointment. Shame is emotional exhaustion with no outlet. Shame is the misunderstanding of a wounded heart.

Women do not feel shame because they did something wrong. Women feel shame because they were harmed and then left to manage the consequences alone.

Shame makes mothers misinterpret their own hearts. Shame convinces a woman that her reactions reflect her character. They don't.

Reactions reflect wounds.

Shame says, "You snapped; you're mean." But truth says, "You snapped; you're hurting."

Shame says, "You're distant; you're cold." But truth says, "You're distant; you're overwhelmed."

Shame says, "You're impatient; you're broken." Truth says, "You're impatient; you're exhausted."

Shame says, "You're inconsistent; you're failing." Truth says, "You were never meant to do this alone."

Shame interprets the symptoms as identity. Truth interprets the symptoms as injury.

Women see failure. God sees fatigue. Women see weakness. God sees wounds. Women see guilt. God sees grief.

Women see themselves. God sees the part of them that is trying to survive.

Shame disconnects women from their children. Not because they don't love their children, but because they feel unworthy of being loved. When shame is present, mothers may withdraw, hide emotionally, avoid affection, overcompensate, become overly strict, feel constantly judged, feel insecure in their parenting. They fear ruining their child, as well, they fear the child seeing their weaknesses and they feel like the child deserves someone better.

These feelings are not truth. They are shame speaking in the mother's voice. The child does not want perfection. The child wants presence. The child does not seek performance. The child seeks connection. The child does not need a flawless parent. The child needs a safe one. A safe parent is a healing parent, not a perfect one.

Shame breaks when women see themselves through god's eyes. God does not look at mothers through the lens of their reactions. He looks at them through the reality of their wounds.

God sees the tears they didn't have time to cry, the nights they stayed awake thinking of solutions. He looks on the heaviness they carried in silence, the sacrifices no one acknowledged. the emotional battles they fought alone. the way they kept showing up despite heartbreak. the love they gave even when they were empty. the way they put their child first even when the father did not. the resilience they didn't recognize in themselves.

God never shames wounded women.

- He heals them.
- He comforts them.
- He restores them.
- He lifts them.
- He defends them.
- He covers them.
- He affirms them.
- He strengthens them.
- He reorders their identity so shame cannot speak anymore.

Shame is broken by truth, not in hiding. If it continually hidden it will remain. What you resist persists. Women often try to fix themselves to escape shame: "I'll be more patient." "I'll be more loving." "I won't react next time." "I'll hold it together. "I'll be strong." But shame isn't healed by performance. Shame is healed by revelation.

The revelation is this:

Your reactions came from pain, not from lack of love. Pain and love co-exist in motherhood. Women can love deeply and hurt deeply at the same time. Truth breaks shame because truth reconnects the mother with her real heart. A heart that loves, that has tried, that has carried too much—God wants to heal that heart. A heart that carried too much, that deserves healing, that's a heart that God wants to restore fully.

A mother cannot heal while feeling condemned. Condemnation paralyzes. Shame suffocates. Guilt isolates. Self-blame drains. All of these block healing. So, before God addresses patterns, before He addresses wounds, before He brings restoration— He breaks shame. He lifts the weight. He silences the accusations. He restores dignity. He reveals innocence. He separates identity from reaction. He brings the woman back to emotional safety. Because healing flows where shame no longer rages or reigns.

The mother is not the source of the problem — she is the key to the solution. Everything changes when shame lifts. The heart softens, the spirit opens, the child feels safer, the home grows lighter, the pattern begins to break, compassion returns, connection deepens, healing accelerates, the past loses its grip. This chapter breaks the internal chains that have held women hostage for years.

It prepares the heart for the next revelation.

CHAPTER 11

The Enemy's Oldest Strategy: Divide the Family

How the Enemy Targets the Mother's Heart After the Father Leaves

The enemy does not need storms, disasters, or dramatic events to destroy a family. He only needs *division*. Division is subtle. Division is quiet. Division is psychological. Division is spiritual. Division is emotional.

And the enemy's oldest strategy is simple: Break the relationship between the parents, then attack the heart of the mother, so the relationship between the mother and child becomes strained.

If the enemy can fracture the foundation, he can distort everything built on it. He knows the mother carries the emotional tone of the home, the child absorbs the mother's emotional state. He knows and is counting on the father's absence leaving a vacuum. that vacuum becomes the battlefield. And the enemy plants thoughts, lies, fears, and emotional triggers in that vacuum.

Not because the mother is weak, but because the mother is *central*. Whoever reaches the mother's heart reaches the home. A woman is designed to multiply, so whatever she receives, it will be multiplied, it will be magnified; she is built that way.

The strategy begins with the father's absence. The enemy uses the father's absence as a spiritual opportunity. When the father is absent, unstable, inconsistent, emotionally unavailable, irresponsible, distant, passive, dismissive, immature his absence becomes a doorway.

And through that doorway, the enemy whispers, "You're alone." "You're unsupported." "You're abandoned." "You're rejected." "You're unlovable." "You're unprotected." "You're overwhelmed." "You're failing." "You're doing everything yourself." "No one sees your pain." And the devil will add to all that by saying, "And you will fail."

These whispers are not thoughts, they are **strategies**. Because if the enemy can destabilize the mother emotionally, he can destabilize what is left of the fragmented family spiritually.

Whether the father is there or not, but especially when he is not, the enemy knows the mother is the emotional gatekeeper. The mother is the thermostat of the home. Her emotional state becomes the child's experience, the atmosphere, the tone, the climate, the energy of the household, the foundation of every interaction. So, the enemy's goal is not merely to hurt her—, but to influence her emotional environment.

If he can overwhelm her, make her doubt herself, drain her emotionally, make her feel ashamed, ignite resentment, stir old wounds, make her distrust affection, attach her emotions to memories of the father, then he can create an emotional tension between mother and child. Not because she doesn't love her child— but because her heart is under spiritual siege.

The enemy uses familiar spirits of the father-wound. The enemy often triggers emotions connected to the father, such as abandonment, betrayal, disappointment, resentment, bitterness, fear, insecurity, anger, and emotional numbness. These emotions get activated by stress, the child's behavior, financial pressure, exhaustion, loneliness, anniversaries of painful events, the child resembling the father, or other memories that resurface unexpectedly. Especially in seasons where support is lacking, the enemy doesn't need new weapons; he reuses the father's wounds as spiritual bait.

All the while, the mother thinks she is reacting to life, when she is actually reacting to emotional triggers the enemy stirred up. Same tricks--, new day.

The goal is always the same: disconnection; a disconnected mother is vulnerable. A disconnected child is unprotected. A disconnected home is spiritually exposed. So, the enemy tries to create emotional distance, irritation, shame, guilt, misunderstanding, mistrust, miscommunication, emotional fatigue emotional shutdown, increased triggers, repeated patterns, unexplainable tension.

His goal is not to make the mother abusive. His goal is to make her discouraged. A discouraged mother is easier to isolate. An isolated mother is easier to influence. An influenced mother is easier to exhaust. An exhausted mother is easier to divide from her child. This is spiritual warfare disguised as emotional struggle.

The enemy only attacks where there is purpose. The enemy does not waste energy. He targets families with destiny, mothers with strong spiritual potential, children with prophetic identity, households God wants to use, bloodlines God intends to heal, and or generational cycles God is breaking. The attacks are evidence of purpose, not evidence of failure.

The enemy sees legacy. He sees the child's calling. He sees the mother's capacity. He sees the lineage being restored. So, he attacks where the future is bright. He attacks where God is building something generational.

He attacks the mother because the mother carries the blueprint and she is spending the most time with the child. The father may be out in the streets living his life seeming unbothered.

But the enemy cannot win against a healing heart. The enemy's strategy fails when the mother recognizes the pattern, the mother understands the emotional triggers, the mother sees the spiritual roots. The mother breaks shame. The mother confronts bitterness. The mother closes emotional doors. The mother separates the child from the father's wounds. The mother invites God into hidden chambers of her heart. Once the mother heals, the enemy loses access.

He cannot use old wounds that no longer hurt. He cannot use old memories that have been redeemed. He cannot use old patterns that have been broken. He cannot use old insecurities that have been replaced with truth. He cannot divide a home that has been spiritually restored.

A healed mother is spiritually dangerous. A healed home is spiritually fortified. A healed child is spiritually protected. A healed lineage is spiritually unbreakable.

This chapter marks the end of the enemy's influence and the beginning of emotional and spiritual reclaiming. This chapter transitions us into healing mode. Now that we have named the enemy's strategy, the next chapters move into the **repair work**—the rebuilding of the mother's heart and the restoration of the mother-child connection.

Healing the Wound of Abandonment

How God Restores What the Father Broke or Left Undone

Abandonment is not just something that *happens* — it is something a woman *carries*. She carries it in her nervous system, even in her sleep patterns. She carries it in her expectations. She carries it in her emotional posture, in her chattiness or silence. She carries it in her parenting. She carries it in her best days and worst days--, in her best or worst moments. Util it is healed and dismissed completely; it is always there.

Abandonment becomes a weight the heart tries to hide, a bruise only she can feel, a hollow space where partnership was supposed to exist. But God never designed a woman to carry this alone. God never intended her to survive what broke her.
He intended her to heal from it.

And healing starts the moment she realizes:

> **"This wound was not my fault,
> but it is in my heart —
> and God wants to restore it."**

Abandonment isn't only the father leaving — it's everything he didn't do. Abandonment can take many forms: For example, he stayed physically but left emotionally, he provided financially but not relationally, he loved the idea of family but not the responsibility. he chose new relationships over stability. He was present but passive. He was connected to the child but disconnected from the mother. He was inconsistent. He was unpredictable. He was immature. He was absent during pregnancy. He was absent in the early years. He returned only when convenient. He created chaos the mother had to clean up. He created children without creating fatherhood. He gave hope but delivered disappointment.

Abandonment is not a single action; it is a lifestyle of absence. And every absence leaves a mark.

God sees every mark.

Abandonment Creates a Double Wound. A mother experiences two emotional injuries:

1. The wound toward the man. "I trusted you." "I loved you." "We created a life together." "I carried the responsibility alone." "You left me to survive what we both created." "You said…. But you changed." "You chose something else over us."

2. The wound toward herself. "Why wasn't I enough?" "Why did this happen to me?" "What did I miss?" "What's wrong with me?" "Why didn't he stay?" "Did I choose wrong?" These two wounds twist together. They form the deepest part of the abandonment injury.

They shape how a woman sees motherhood, relationships, and herself.

God gently untangles these wounds — layer by layer. **God** heals the wound by restoring truth. Abandonment teaches lies. God confronts every lie with truth. **Lie:** "I was not enough." **Truth:** *You were more than enough — he was unhealed.*

Lie: "I'm hard to love."
Truth: *You loved too deeply for someone who wasn't ready.*

Lie: "I was foolish."
Truth: *You were sincere — he was broken.*

Lie: "I must have missed the signs."
Truth: *You were hopeful — he was inconsistent.*

Lie: "Maybe I deserved this."
Truth: *No one deserves abandonment — it is a reflection of the father's wounds, not yours.*

Lie: "I'm carrying this weight because I failed."
Truth: *You are carrying this weight because he abandoned his role—he failed.*

When God restores Truth, the trauma and the wound both lose their power.

God heals the wound by filling the empty places. The father left emotional holes, financial, relational, spiritual and generational holes. His voids will be felt until the Lord heals. God can heal all those and the protective holes, identity holes, and partnership holes.

God fills each one.

Maybe not at once, even though sometimes deliverance can be immediate, but God is faithful, consistent, gentle and soul restoration and prosperity sometimes takes time.

God steps into the roles the father abandoned. Where the father did not protect —
God becomes the shield.

Where the father did not support —
God becomes the provider.

Where the father did not show affection —
God becomes the source of love.

Where the father created insecurity —
God becomes stability.

Where the father caused fear —
God becomes safety.

Where the father shattered trust —
God rebuilds trust from the inside out.

Where the father broke her heart —
God restores her identity.

Where the father left gaps —
God fills them with glory.

Healing is not replacing the child's father, it's replacing the wound with God's presence.

God heals the wound by disconnecting the child from the father's actions. This is one of the most miraculous parts of healing. When the mother heals, the child becomes spiritually and emotionally free from the consequences of the father's mistakes.

Through healing, God breaks generational pain, emotional residue, subconscious resentment, inherited fear, internalized rejection. God breaks and heals the echo of the father's absence, the emotional weight that the child never deserved, and the rejection shadow that followed the child from birth.

God does not only heal the mother, but He also restores the child. The mother's healing becomes the child's inheritance. Abandonment steals a woman's sense of self. It changes her confidence, joy, openness, trust, vulnerability, ability to rest, emotional softness. God heals by giving the mother back to herself. Healing gives all of it back.

A healed woman is lighter, kinder to herself, more patient, more affectionate, more confident, more emotionally present, more spiritually aware, more connected to her child, less reactive, less fearful, less triggered, less guarded. Healing doesn't make a woman perfect; it makes her *herself again* while God is right there offering her factory re-sets to the version she lost. The version she forgot. The version abandonment tried to erase. The version God never stopped seeing. to make her who she once was, he also is offering increase, promotion, and soul prosperity for her very being. It's like when Jesus healed the 10 lepers but only one came back thankful and that leper was made whole. We should all seek for *wholeness*. And it is possible, in God.

Healing the wound of abandonment breaks the generational pattern. When a woman heals from abandonment her reactions change, her expectations soften, her heart opens, her tone shifts, her presence deepens, her child becomes more secure, her home feels safer and her emotional world stabilizes.

Healing doesn't just rewrite her story — it rewrites her child's story. And that is the beauty of God; He restores what the father broke by healing the heart of the mother and protecting the destiny of the child because as we all know, God has a vested interest in each of us reaching destiny.

CHAPTER 13

Releasing the Man (Even If He Never Apologizes)

Breaking Emotional and Spiritual Ties to His Actions

A woman can move on physically but still be tied emotionally. She can leave the relationship but still carry the wound. She can raise the child alone but still feel the father's shadow in the house. She can say she's "over it" and still be triggered by his name, his choices, his inconsistency, his irresponsibility, his presence on social media, or even the resemblance she sees in the child.

Releasing the man is not the same as forgiving him. Forgiveness deals with the offense. Release deals with the *attachment*. Forgiveness says, "I let this go." Release says, "You no longer have emotional power in my life." Both are different. Both are needed. Both set the mother free.

Most importantly, **release is not for the man. Release is for the woman and the child.** Women may hesitate to release because they think "He doesn't deserve it." But release is necessary, even if the man is wrong, wrong, wrong. It can't be justified with, "He caused this." "He didn't apologize." "He hasn't changed." "He's still irresponsible." "He's still doing damage." "He keeps hurting our child."

All of this may be true. But release is not about *him*. Release is about *you*. Release means, he cannot drain your emotions anymore. He cannot shape your parenting anymore, he cannot trigger your heart anymore, he cannot influence the atmosphere of your home anymore. He cannot dictate your moods anymore, he cannot control your peace anymore, he cannot be the unspoken presence in your reactions, he cannot be the reference point for your wounds, he cannot be the spiritual doorway into your home.

Release is an act of spiritual authority, not emotional surrender. You are not freeing him. You are freeing yourself.

Release does not excuse him — it extracts you. Many women fear that releasing the man feels like letting him off the hook, thereby minimizing what he did, ignoring the damage. Pretending he didn't cause pain, acting like everything is fine. But release is none of those things.

Release is:

"I am removing you from the center of my emotional world."

"You no longer get access to my peace."

"Your choices no longer define my reactions."

"Your absence no longer controls my presence."

"Your wound will not shape my motherhood."

"You will not be the reason I cannot bond with my child."

Release is not leniency. This is liberation. Release is you taking your heart back from a man who mishandled it. Release means ending the emotional contract. Every relationship creates an invisible emotional contract. When the relationship ends, the contract often remains open emotionally, even if it is closed physically.

The contract says, "I am still angry at you." "You still owe me." "I deserved better." "You hurt me." "You should have stayed." "You should have helped." "You should have grown up." "You should have been a partner." "You should have supported this child." "You should have matured by now."

Every "should" is an emotional tie. Every "should" becomes a spiritual tether. Every "should" keeps the man present in the home, even when he is gone. Release closes the emotional contract. Not because he fulfilled it, but because God is taking over the terms.

Release makes space for God to heal the mother-child bond. When a man takes up emotional space in a woman's heart through bitterness, resentment, pain, disappointment, or hopes that have not died — he takes up emotional space in her motherhood.

Release clears that space. When release happens, the mother sees the child clearly, the child no longer carries the residue of the father, the child is freed from emotional substitution. The mother's patience increases, the mother's tone softens. Triggers decrease, resentment dissolves. The home becomes lighter. The emotional atmosphere resets, the mother-child bond becomes stronger. Releasing the man is one of the greatest gifts a woman can give her child.

Because release ends the emotional inheritance of the father's dysfunction.

Releasing the man requires no participation from him. He does not need to apologize, mature, change, agree, understand, take responsibility, be involved, show remorse, become better, do his part, cooperate in any way. Release is a spiritual act done privately, between a woman and God.

The man has nothing to do with it. He cannot block it. He cannot delay it. He cannot undo it. Release is a divine transaction where God removes the emotional weight the woman has carried and replaces it with Peace.

The Holy Spirit leads the release gently. Release does not happen all at once. It happens in layers:

• **Layer 1: Naming the Wound** - "This hurt me."

• **Layer 2: Naming the Truth** - "This was not my fault."

- **Layer 3: Separating the Child From the Pain -** "This is not about my child."

- **Layer 4: Separating Myself From His Actions -** "What he did does not define me."

- **Layer 5: Surrendering the Emotional Hooks -** "I am letting go of the need for closure."

- **Layer 6: Giving the Weight to God -** "God, take this burden from my heart."

- **Layer 7: Receiving Peace -** "I accept Your healing." Release is not forgetting. Release is not pretending. Release is not erasing. Release is **letting God heal the parts of your heart the man wounded**.

A released woman is a free woman. This is what release looks like she no longer reacts when she hears his name. She no longer rehearses old conversations. She no longer imagines what "should have been." She no longer matches the child's behavior with the father's personality. She no longer feels resentment on birthdays, holidays, or anniversaries. She no longer carries bitterness, she no longer feels heaviness around the child, she no longer feels entangled. she no longer feels ashamed. She no longer feels the emotional drain; she can love freely again. Her heart returns to fullness. Her emotions return to balance. Her peace becomes stronger than her pain.

A released woman is spiritually unshakeable, emotionally stable, and deeply connected to her child.

Now that the emotional tie to the man is broken, the next chapter restores the mother's ability to see the child clearly, without the father's shadow.

CHAPTER 14

Reframing the Child

Seeing the Child as Themselves, Not as the Father's Echo

When the emotional tie to the father is active, the child becomes a reflection of him — not intentionally, not consciously, but emotionally. Everything the child does filters through the mother's history with the man. A child's stubbornness resembles his resistance. A child's silence resembles his withdrawal. A child's mistakes resemble his irresponsibility. A child's tone resembles his disrespect. A child's neediness resembles his demands. A child's independence resembles his detachment.

A child's personality resembles his flaws. A child's behavior resembles his unhealed wounds. The child becomes a canvas of a relationship the mother survived. Not because the child is doing anything wrong — but because the father's echoes are still in the atmosphere. But once the mother releases the man, the child becomes visible again. Not as an echo. Not as a reminder. Not as a symbol. Not as a resemblance. Not as a carrying case for the father's mistakes. The child becomes **themselves** --a soul with identity. That small person becomes a life with purpose, a person with their own spirit. They show up as children with their own future. Someone God designed entirely apart from the man who fathered them.

This chapter is about reclaiming that truth.

The child is not the father — even if they resemble him. Children inherit DNA, not dysfunction. They may look like him, walk like him, talk like him, smile like him. frown like him, mimic his mannerisms, carry his physical features. share his temperamental traits. But they do **not** carry his immaturity, his irresponsibility, his emotional instability, his brokenness, his spiritual issues, his choices, his dysfunction, his abandonment, his wounds, his rejection, his sins. A mother must separate resemblance from identity.

Resemblance comes from biology. Identity comes from God. The father contributed genes. God contributed destiny. The child's identity is divine, not inherited through trauma.

Reframing the child begins with seeing them without pain. When pain is present, every interaction becomes charged, A child's question becomes a demand. A child's mistake becomes disrespect. A child's emotion becomes manipulation. A child's independence becomes rebellion. A child's curiosity becomes defiance. A child's fear becomes weakness. A child's silliness becomes irritation. A woman's patience is worn thin in all this pain because she is using it all up on herself--, just to cope, just to get by, just to function or to at least look like she is functioning.

But when pain lifts, what should be adorable childish behaviors return to what they really are: questions, mistakes, emotions, independence, curiosity, fear, silliness. Your kid is a kid; don't rob them of their childhood and don't let that *daddy* that you're mad at, absent or present, rob them either.

Normal childhood. Not father echoes. A healed lens sees "My child is growing, not provoking." "My child is learning, not resisting." "My child is human, not *him*." "My child is innocent, not triggering." "My child is separate from my story." This reframing is the beginning of pure connection.

A mother must learn the child's personality without the father's shadow. A healed mother studies her child like a new person, not a reminder. She begins to ask "Who is my child?" "What is their temperament?" "How do they express love?" "How do they handle fear?" "What triggers them?" "What comforts them?" "What makes them feel *seen*?" "How do they learn?" "What makes them unique?" "What spiritual gifts do they carry?" "What does God say about them?" Now, that's parenting, that's giving the gift of learning a new person from the beginning and not pre-judging thinking you know them already saying, "You're just like your daddy," and rejecting them.

That's not fair. But you know that, *right*?

She discovers that much of what she once interpreted negatively was simply personality, developmental stage, temperament, emotional growth, communication style, immaturity, need for guidance, stress response, natural uniqueness. Nothing to do with the father. Everything to do with the child's individuality.

When the child is reframed, the relationship heals instantly. The healing is immediate because the child senses the shift. A reframed child feels, safer, understood, valued, loved without conflict, free to express themselves, free to make mistakes, free to ask questions, free to grow, free to be imperfect, free to be a child, They no longer walk on emotional eggshells. They no longer feel blamed. They no longer feel like the mother's mood depends on their behavior. They no longer unfairly carry the father's mistakes in mother's eyes. They no longer feel emotionally responsible. The atmosphere becomes clearer. The connection becomes deeper. Eye contact becomes easier. The affection becomes natural. The tension dissolves. The mother no longer feels triggered. The child no longer feels misunderstood. They finally meet each other heart-to-heart instead of pain-to-behavior.

Reframing requires emotional separation from the father. A mother can only see the child clearly when the father is no longer in the emotional center, his wounds are no longer active triggers, his behavior is no longer shaping her responses, his absence is no longer the defining emotion, his past is no longer interrupting her present, his voice is no longer louder than God's. Hear this: the man is finally demoted from idol status! Once this separation occurs, the child becomes a blessing, not a burden. A person, not a reminder. A joy, not a trigger. A divine assignment, not an emotional substitution.

God loves to reveal the child's true identity to the mother. God waits for this moment. As soon as the emotional fog clears, He begins to show the mother, the child's spiritual gifts. the child's sensitivity, the child's strengths. God reveals the child's innocence, their divine purpose and personality, the child's emotional needs, the child's heart, their potential. He reveals that the child is **not that man**; the child is their own person. He reveals that the child carries heaven's imprint, not the father's wounds. He reveals that the child was chosen *by God*, not by the man. And the healed mother finally sees that.

God has always seen "my child is separate." "my child is pure." "my child is not the father." "my child is my assignment, not my reminder." This revelation transforms motherhood.

Reframing sets the stage for restoration. Once the child is reframed, resentment dissolves, bitterness loses its target, guilt disappears, shame is lifted, emotional substitution ends, triggers stop activating, the mother-child bond strengthens, the household atmosphere becomes peaceful. Reframing is deliverance. It is revelation. It is restoration.

CHAPTER 15

Parenting From a Healed Place

Practical, Emotional, and Spiritual Tools for a New Kind of Motherhood

When a mother heals, her parenting changes — not because she tries harder, but because she is *lighter*. A healed heart reacts differently. A healed mind interprets differently. A healed spirit leads differently. A healed mother loves differently.

This chapter is the bridge between revelation and daily life — between *understanding the wound* and *living from wholeness*. Parenting from a healed place is not about perfection. It is about **presence**. It is about showing up with clarity instead of confusion, with tenderness instead of tension, with wisdom instead of emotional exhaustion, with compassion instead of resentment, with patience instead of triggers. It is where motherhood becomes peaceful again.

1. The Healed Mother Has an Emotional Reset. A healed mother becomes emotionally present in ways she could not be before. Not because she suddenly has more energy —but because she no longer leaks energy into old wounds. Her emotional space clears. She begins to respond instead of react, listen instead of defend, see instead of assume, guide instead of overcorrect, breathe instead of tighten, comfort instead of withdraw, engage instead of shut down, love without fear of being drained, Her presence feels different — not only to the child, but to herself., She no longer feels weighed down by motherhood. She feels *connected* to it.

2. The Healed Mother Establishes New Rhythms

Healing makes everyday parenting easier because internal pressure decreases. She becomes intentional about her tone. It is softer, not forced — it flows naturally. She may now take short pauses before responding, A moment to breathe breaks old patterns. Her eye contact now signals safety and availability instead of "Boy, you are going to get it!" She now has a gentler physical touch. All these changes restore connection and communicates warmth. Short, clear instructions. Removes tension and decreases frustration. She now employs calm consequences for discipline instead of reactive, or violent punishments.

Daily emotional check-ins are good such as: "You good? Anything on your mind?" Predictable routines, Healing thrives in structure. These small shifts transform the home without dramatic effort.

3. The Healed Mother Communicates with Clarity Instead of Emotion. When unhealed, mothers often communicate from exhaustion, frustration, resentment, overwhelm, fear, triggers, exasperation or anxiety. Healed, mothers communicate from confidence, peace,

clarity, gentleness, purpose, calm authority. The child feels the difference immediately. Communication becomes kinder, softer, more direct, less emotional, less reactive, more purposeful and more nurturing. The mother no longer accuses the child as to why she and the home are not peaceful. The home is peaceful because *she* is healed.

4. The Healed Mother Uses Affirmation as a Spiritual Weapon. Affirmation is not flattery. It is identity-shaping. When a mother heals, her words carry different power. She begins speaking to who the child *is*, not who she fears they will become. Affirmations like "You are loved." "You are safe with me." "You're not like him — you're your own person." "I enjoy you." "You have a good heart." "I'm proud of you." "You're growing beautifully." "I like the person you are becoming." "You are chosen by God." "You are my blessing, not my burden."

These words rewrite the child's internal world. They heal fractures the child could never articulate. They create emotional stability. They rewire the child's sense of identity. A mother's affirmation is emotional architecture.

5. The Healed Mother Responds Instead of Reacts. A practical shift

Reaction: instant, emotional, often intensified by triggers.

Response: intentional, calm, connected to logic and love. A healed mother gains the ability to pause.

That pause is healing in action.

She begins to ask herself "Is this about the child or about my day?" "Is this about now or about my past?" "Am I reacting to their behavior or to my memories?" "Is my tone reflecting fear or love?" "What does my child actually need right now?" These questions create emotional clarity. The child no longer receives displaced emotion. They receive appropriate guidance.

6. The Healed Mother Practices Micro-Affection. Small gestures build strong bonds. Healing frees a woman to touch the child's shoulder when passing, hug without heaviness, kiss the child on the forehead before school, sit close while watching a show, laugh freely with the child, hold their hand when crossing the parking lot, stroke their back during a hard moment, speak softly when correcting, listen fully without multitasking. These tiny acts create massive emotional safety.

7. The Healed Mother Disciplines with Connection, Not Control. Discipline becomes calm, consistent, emotionally safe, separate from shame, specific to behavior, not identity. She no longer tries to "fix" the child. She guides. She no longer parents out of fear. She parents out of confidence. She no longer uses harshness. She uses clarity. She no longer withdraws affection. She maintains connection. Discipline becomes an expression of love, not frustration.

8. The Healed Mother Gives the Child Permission to Be Human. This is a major shift. A healed mother allows mistakes, understands childish immaturity (in a child), welcomes emotions, responds to tears with compassion, accepts that growth is messy, doesn't personalize the child's behavior, separates development from defiance, expects age-appropriate challenges, and doesn't interpret childhood through adult logic. When the mother stops seeing the child as the father's echo, she no longer expects perfection or fears resemblance.

She lets the child be what they truly are-- a growing human who needs unconditional love.

9. The Healed Mother Builds a Spiritual Covering Over the Home. Healing makes room for God to dwell. She starts to pray out loud again, bless the child intentionally, speak Scripture over the home, play worship softly in the background, pray peace over the mornings, pray protection over the nights, pray identity over the child, pray healing over her own heart, pray clarity over her reactions. Spiritual covering is necessary. Ideally the father should have brought that, but since he is not there, the mom has to step up.

Parenting from a healed place becomes lighter, calmer, more joyful, deeply bonding, spiritually aligned, emotionally safe, gentler, more intuitive, less exhausting, more fulfilling, The mother is no longer leading from survival. She is leading from restoration.

Her healed heart is her child's inheritance.

CHAPTER 16

Undoing Years of Emotional Transfer

How to Rebuild Connection With a Child You've Unconsciously Wounded

Even the best mothers wound their children unintentionally. Not because they lack love, but because they lack support, healing, partnership, and peace. Emotional transfer is what happens when a mother is hurting and the child receives the overflow of that hurt.

Some children receive sharp tones, side eyes or glaring looks, emotional withdrawal, impatience, irritation, unfair discipline, minimal affection, emotional distance, unpredictable reactions, as well as resentment that wasn't theirs to carry. Children internalize all of it as "mom is hurting," but as "Something is wrong with me." Or, "I make mom upset." "Mom is unhappy because of me." "I'm the cause of the tension." "I'm not lovable." "I need to be more perfect." "I should stay quiet." "I have to make mom proud." "I have to earn love." Or "I should avoid her." "I should shut down." "I shouldn't ask for comfort." This chapter is not about guilt. This chapter is about repair. Because God restores what the mother regrets. and heals what the child endured.

1. Repair Begins with Recognition, Not Condemnation. A healed mother can look backward without drowning in guilt. She can say "I see where I was hurting." "I see how the child was affected." "I didn't know." "I wasn't malicious." "I was overwhelmed." "I was wounded." "I was doing everything alone." "I didn't have support." "I couldn't give what I never received." "But now I'm healing." Thank You, Jesus.

This recognition is powerful. It ends shame. It opens the door to restoration. It creates emotional clarity. A mother who sees the past clearly can change the future completely.

2. Repair Is Not an Apology — It's a Reconnection. Children need repair, not perfection. Apology says "I'm sorry for how I acted." Repair says: "I'm here now, fully present." Apology acknowledges the event. Repair restores the bond. Children don't need long speeches. Children need softness, warmth, safety, consistency, affection, predictable calm, and attuned presence. A healed mother begins showing up in ways the child always needed. The child begins to heal simply by feeling the difference.

3. Name the Emotion Without Blame. A repaired connection begins when the mother can verbalize moments like "I was tired, and I reacted harshly. That wasn't your fault." Or "I was overwhelmed that day. You didn't do anything wrong." Or "Mom was hurting back then. I see how that affected you, and I'm so sorry."

This is not shame. This is liberation. Children experience emotional clarity for the first time. The confusion lifts. The internal narrative changes. They no longer feel responsible for the mother's wounds.

4. Offer What Was Missing — Without Forcing It

Children heal when a mother gives them:

• **More affection** - A gentle hug, a hand squeeze, or a soft touch.

• **More attention** - Being fully present without multitasking.

• **More patience** - Letting them speak without rushing.

• **More curiosity** - Asking about their feelings, not just their behavior.

• **More softness** - Responding with calm even when they misbehave.

• **More emotional safety** - Creating an environment where crying or frustration is safe.

• **More empathy** - Understanding their fears and frustrations.

• **More joy** - Laughing together, creating playful moments.

These small adjustments are monumental. They repair neural pathways. They heal emotional beliefs. They rebuild trust. They create warmth. Children thrive on consistency, not intensity. Small acts, repeated, become healing.

5. Create New Emotional Patterns. The mother begins building a different emotional world for the child. This may show up as more calm mornings, peaceful corrections, gentle tone, soft eye contact, deliberate affection, slow, patient answers, intentional listening, predictable routines, emotionally safe responses, These create a new foundation. Children feel it instantly. A home that was once tense becomes a place of refuge.

Children begin to relax. They smile more freely. They express emotion without fear. They approach the mother with confidence. The past loses its power. The present becomes healing. The future becomes whole.

6. For Older Children: The Repair May Be Slower but Deeper. Older children may withdraw, test the new boundaries, question the changes. respond cautiously, look for inconsistencies, protect their hearts, fear disappointment. This is normal. his is not rejection. This is self-protection.

A healed mother responds with patience, quiet consistency, emotional honesty, stable affection, predictable calm. Over time, the older child sees that "Mom is different." "She's safer now." "I can trust her again." "She's not reacting like before." "She hears me." "She sees me." "She understands me."

Older children heal more slowly, but they heal more deeply.

7. Pray Over the Wounds You Cannot See

Prayer touches what conversation cannot. A mother can pray, "Lord, heal the places my words cannot reach." "Restore the parts of my child's heart that absorbed my pain." "Remove every emotional weight they carried for me." "Break every residue of fear, burden, or confusion." "Release peace into every memory." "Fill them with security where they once felt uncertainty." These prayers become spiritual surgery. God enters the emotional spaces the mother cannot physically touch and heals the child from the inside out.

8. Show Up Differently — But Consistently

Consistency is the miracle. Children heal when today's tone matches yesterday's tone, affection matches the apology, connection remains steady, the atmosphere stays safe, the reactions stay calm, the mother's heart stays open. Consistency proves that the change is real. Consistency rewrites the child's emotional expectations. Consistency builds trust. Consistency is love in action.

Undoing Years of Emotional Transfer Creates a New Legacy. When emotional transfer ends the child regains innocence, the mother regains joy, the home regains peace, the generational cycle is broken, the emotional atmosphere resets, the connection becomes strong, the trauma stops here.

CHAPTER 17

The Child That God Sent — Not the Man

Why the Child's Purpose Is Independent of the Father's Failure

There is a moment in every mother's healing where she finally realizes **"My child came *through* the man, but not *from* the man."** This revelation breaks a thousand unspoken burdens at once. It separates the child from the father's sins, from the father's absence, from the father's identity. And also, from the father's immaturity, failures, brokenness, and from the father's choices.

DNA is not destiny. Biology is not calling. And *resemblance is not identity.*

The child was sent by **God, not the man and ultimately belongs to God.** You will have to give account to God as to how you raised this small person that He entrusted to you, The man was simply the human vessel. A biological door. A temporary participant in a divine assignment. The father had a moment. God had a plan. And the plan is what lives inside the child.

1. The Child's Purpose Was Written Before the Relationship Existed. Before the two adults ever met, before the attraction, before the romance, before the pain, before the pregnancy, before the disappointment. God had already written the child's destiny, designed their personality, chosen their gifts, shaped their spiritual identity, mapped their future, placed a calling on their life, determined their purpose, sealed their life with intention. The child is a divine assignment, not an accidental outcome. Even if the relationship was wrong, the child was always right. People can be mismatched but God never misplaces children.

2. A Father Can Fail the Mother and Still Not Interrupt the Calling

This is one of the mysteries of God's goodness. The father's failure cannot cancel the child's future, the child's anointing, the child's talents, the child's emotional capacity, the child's gifts, the child's spiritual covering, the child's purpose, nor the child's divine favor. Human failure cannot interrupt divine intention. The father can break the relationship, but he cannot break the calling. The father can abandon his role, but he cannot cancel God's plan. Because the plan never came from him.

3. The Enemy Tried to Attach the Father's Identity to the Child.
The enemy wanted the child to feel unwanted, abandoned, inferior, insecure, unworthy, feel father-shaped shame, feel responsible for the mother's pain, or feel like a reminder instead of a blessing. But God interrupts this assignment through revelation.

When the mother realizes: "My child is not his mistakes," every spiritual attack against the child loses its foundation. When the mother realizes: "My child is God-sent," and starts praying in earnest, she stops facilitating every generational curse breaks that is opposing her child.

The child becomes spiritually unreachable by the father's dysfunction because they are fully rooted in God's purpose.

4. The Child Has Their Own Personality, Separate From Both Parents. A child is more than genetics, traits, tendencies, inherited patterns. Children carry **originality**. God did not copy the father when He designed the child. He created someone new. A new spirit. A new soul. A new future. A new identity. A new purpose. A unique destiny.

What you see in your child is not the father resurfacing —, it is God's creativity unfolding. Some traits resemble the man. But the *essence* of the child comes from God.

5. The Child Was Not Sent to Punish the Mother

Many women suffer silently with thoughts like "Why did this happen to me?" "Why did I have a child with him?" "Why was I chosen for this?" "Why did I have to raise this child alone?" "Why did God let this happen?" These thoughts come from survival, not from truth.

The truth is The child was not punishment. The child was purpose. The child was not an accident. The child was an assignment. The child was not a consequence. The child was a calling. The child was not a mistake. The child was a miracle.

God does not punish women with children —
He blesses the world through them.

6. The Mother Was Chosen, Not Burdened

The relationship may have been painful. The circumstances may have been unfair. The father may have failed. But the mother was selected. God chose *her* womb. God chose *her* strength. God chose *her* capacity. God chose *her* resilience. God chose *her* spirit. God chose *her* tenderness. God chose *her* heart. The father was a doorway. The mother is the destiny.

7. Once the Mother Sees the Child's God-Given Identity, Everything Changes

Her tone changes. Her interactions shift. Her heart opens. Her healing deepens. Her patience expands. Her resentment dissolves. Her affection increases. Her perspective transforms. She begins to say, "This is God's child." "This child is assigned to me." "This child is not my pain." "This child is not his memory." "This child is not his echo." "This child is an answer, not a question."

This revelation reorders motherhood. It resets the atmosphere of the home. It heals the child's internal world. It breaks spiritual inheritance. It silences generational patterns. It brings clarity where confusion lived. It brings joy where heaviness lingered. It restores peace where tension once ruled.

The child stands alone, under God, without the father's shadow.

Free.
Whole.
Loved.
Chosen.
Purposed.

This chapter repositions the child in the light of destiny. Now that the child is seen clearly, the next chapter teaches the mother how to actively bless and restore the emotional and spiritual identity of the child.

CHAPTER 18

Blessing the Child You Once Misunderstood

Speaking Life, Purpose, and Identity Over Them

There is nothing more powerful in a child's life than the words spoken by a healed mother. A mother's voice is one of the first sounds a child hears, one of the first voices they trust, one of the strongest forces that shapes their internal world.

Words are not just sounds — they are *assignments*, they are *identity markers*, they are *spiritual seeds*. And when a mother begins to bless the child she once parented under pressure, something sacred happens. Emotional wounds close, the atmosphere shifts, the child's shoulders relax, the child's heart opens, the child becomes more confident. The mother-child bond deepens, guilt dissolves, shame breaks, generational patterns lose their foothold, identity becomes rooted, destiny becomes louder than history.

Blessing is not a ritual. Blessing is restoration.

1. Blessing Replaces the Words Pain Once Spoke

Pain speaks in sharp tones, misunderstandings, impatience, emotional withdrawal, harsh corrections, reactive discipline, misinterpretation, distance, and silence, These were not the mother's true words. These were the wound's words. Now the healed heart speaks instead. Blessing replaces emotional residue with identity. Blessing rewrites the child's emotional dictionary. Blessing cleans the atmosphere. Blessing restores what emotional transfer damaged. Blessing is spiritual reclamation.

2. Children Believe the Voice They Hear Most Often

Before healing, the child may have heard, "Stop." "Hurry up." "I don't have time." "Not now." "What are you doing?" "I told you already." "Why would you do that?" "You're acting like him." "Go sit down." "You always…" "You never…" These were the voice of exhaustion, not the voice of love.

Now the mother replaces the wound's voice with God's voice. And children grow quickly under blessing. They blossom. They break out of fear. They shed old emotional beliefs. Blessing is the sunlight their spirit has always needed.

3. Blessing Speaks to the Child's Identity, Not Their Behavior. Behavior needs correction. Identity needs affirmation. Blessing says, "You have a good heart." "You're growing beautifully." "You are patient." "You are wise." "You are kind." "You are thoughtful." "You are strong." "You are chosen." "You belong." "You are a joy to me." "You are who God created you to be."

These words don't just encourage — they **transform**. Children rise to the level of identity, not the level of correction. When a mother blesses their identity, their behavior begins to align with truth.

4. Blessing Must Be Specific, Not General

Children respond to detail. A general blessing is nice. A specific blessing is healing.

Examples:

Not "You're smart," but "I love how curious you are."

Not "You're good," but "You handled that so kindly."

Not "You're fine," but "It's okay to feel what you feel. I am here."

Not "Be strong," but "You are brave even when something feels scary."

Not "Stop crying," but "Your feelings matter to me."

Not "You're acting like him," but "You are uniquely you. You're nothing like his mistakes."

Details anchor identity.

5. Blessing Must Be Consistent to Undo Old Patterns

Consistency breaks emotional patterns. Daily affirmations, calm tones, repeated encouragement, bedtime blessings, morning blessings, blessings before school, make all the difference to a child—wouldn't those blessings bless you? Bless your child even when they make mistakes, or when they're emotional. Bless them at all times, even when nothing special is happening.

Children heal through repetition.

Every blessing, every repetition builds a home inside them --, a home of confidence. Through your own spoken words you can built a home of security and emotional safety inside your child. A home of identity, acceptance and belonging is one that will bless them and honor you in your old age.

6. Bless the Child Privately and Publicly

Both matter.

Private Blessings:

Restore the child's inner world.
Repair quiet wounds.
Build emotional safety.

Public Blessings:

Affirm value in front of others.
Break shame.
Build external confidence.
Confirm identity.
Teach the child they are worthy of honor.

Examples:

"This is my child. They're brilliant and kind." "I'm proud of who they're becoming." "They're such a blessing."

When a child hears this publicly, something deep inside them stands up straight.

7. Blessing Is Spiritual Warfare

Blessing fights what tried to form the child fear, insecurity, low self-worth, emotional confusion, resentment, rejection, guilt, self-blame, generational patterns. Blessing establishes divine truth over emotional history. When the mother blesses, the enemy loses authority. Blessing is a spiritual decree.

8. A Sample Blessing for the Mother to Speak Over the Child

Here is a blessing that repairs years of emotional misunderstanding:

"I love you.
You are safe.
You are wanted.
You are chosen by God.
You are not the echo of another person —
you are God's original design.
You were never the cause of my pain.
You were never the reason for my tears.
You are a gift to me, not a burden.
You bring joy into my life.
You are growing beautifully.

I bless your mind, your heart, your spirit, and your future.
You belong to God,
and I will love you with a healed and open heart."

Speak this often.
Identity grows through repeated truth.

Blessing Restores What Pain Damaged

This chapter is where healing becomes visible.

The child begins to smile more, relax emotionally, feel secure, engage more, trust the mother, express affection, show vulnerability, express needs, feel protected, behave more confidently, Because the mother's words reshape the inside of the child.

Blessing is generational renovation.

CHAPTER 19

Rewriting the Family Legacy

Stopping Patterns So They Don't Transfer Into the Next Generation

Every family passes something down. Some families pass down joy. Some pass down fear. Some pass down faith. Others, trauma. Some pass down strength. Some pass down brokenness. Some pass down resilience. Some pass down silence. Some pass down emotional intelligence. Some pass down survival. Some pass down abandonment.

But no family escapes inheritance. There is the obvious natural inheritance and there is also bloodline inheritance. We must have awareness and recognize what is in us and what we are passing down to our children. The only question is:

- **What will you continue?**
- **What will you end?**
- **What will you begin?**

This chapter is about shifting your family line—taking the weight of yesterday off your child's shoulders and planting something new for generations after them.

When a mother heals, entire bloodlines shift. When a mother heals from recent hurts, bloodline, generational or ancestral issues, entire bloodlines shift.

1. Generational Patterns Are Not Genetic — They Are Emotional and Spiritual

People often confuse inheritance with inevitability. But generational cycles just don't pass down because of genetics. They pass down because of repeated emotional patterns, unhealed wounds, spiritual open doors, learned behaviors, emotional atmosphere, modeled relationships, internalized beliefs, family silence, unresolved pain, trauma that never got a voice.

Children repeat everything—not just what they feel, but what they're told and even things they overhear. They absorb the emotional climate of the home just as much as they inherit the biological traits of the body. They are targets of nature and nurture.

But the good news is that Emotional and spiritual patterns can be broken the moment someone becomes aware of them. Awareness is deliverance. Healing is inheritance.

2. The Pattern Often Begins With the Father — But It Ends with the Mother.
The father's absence or inconsistency may have started the cycle abandonment, rejection, instability, emotional neglect, irresponsibility, inconsistency, absence during developmental seasons, broken promises, lack of covering, lack of affection.

But the mother's healing is what ends it.

Not because she is responsible for his choices, but because she is the one raising the child. The emotional inheritance comes through whoever is present, not whoever left. And that means, **healing the mother rewrites the child's emotional DNA.**

In this case, the father injured the family line. But the mother restores it.

3. What You Heal, Your Children Won't Have to Fight. This is the miracle of generational healing. When you heal, your child becomes emotionally secure. You healing transforms your child's spiritual groundedness. Because you are healed, your child avoids identity confusion. Your child avoids father-wound patterns. Your child avoids fear-based relationships. Your child avoids low self-worth. Your child avoids perfectionism. Your child avoids people-pleasing. Your child avoids abandonment anxiety. Your child avoids cycles of picking unhealed partners. Your child avoids emotional instability.

Your healing becomes their foundation. Your healing becomes their protection. Your healing becomes their inheritance.

4. You Are the First Healed Mother in Your Line — and That Changes Everything. There is always one person in a family who says, "The pain stops with me." That person becomes the pivot. The hinge. The turnaround point. The generational breaker.

You become the first emotionally present mother the first spiritually aware parent the first to bless intentionally, the first to understand trauma, the first to respond instead of react, the first to separate the child from the father's mistakes, the first to create safety instead of survival, the first to examine your own heart honestly, the first to stop emotional inheritance, the first to partner with God in restoring the family line, Your lineage will remember you, as the one who healed what everyone else endured.

5. Generational Healing Is Intentional, Not Accidental. It does not "just happen." It happens because a mother chooses to bless her child, to heal her wounds, to break bitterness, to release the man, to parent with softness, to speak life, to practice emotional presence, to pray over the home, to create calm, to confront triggers, to change her tone, to choose connection over control, to listen instead of shame, to create safety instead of fear. These choices build a new generational foundation. Healing is built one choice at a time.

All of that seems so hard to do, but staying wounded, angry, and bitter is also hard to do and there are absolutely no good benefits from remaining unhealed.

6. The Child Will Pass Down What You Teach Them — Not What You Survived. Your child will inherit emotional stability, spiritual grounding, self-worth, good communication, emotional availability, secure attachment, a healed mother as their grandmother, generational peace, That means your healing today, sets the emotional climate for people who don't even exist yet.

That is the power of generational healing. When you heal, your grandchildren will grow up in homes where mothers are soft fathers are present (because your child chooses differently), love is consistent, communication is healthy, conflict is safe, affection is normal, emotional intelligence is modeled, prayers are spoken, identity is affirmed, trauma is not inherited.

Your healing reaches into the future.

Important: I am in no way saying that the woman's behavior made the man to leave. Men leave for all kinds of reasons. It could be anything from foundational issues to simple greed, lust, selfishness to actual witchcraft. You walk in healing for yourself. You are healed for your child, not for the purpose of catching or keeping a man.

7. God Honors Mothers Who Heal Generational Lines. God sees the work. God honors the work. God multiplies the work. He sends protection, favor, emotional wisdom, spiritual discernment, restoration, peace, clarity, generational stability, blessings that flow downward. When a mother stands in the gap for her lineage, Heaven stands in the gap with her.

8. Legacy Is Not What You Leave Behind — It's What You Start

Legacy begins the moment you say, "This will not pass to my children." Legacy begins the moment you heal your reactions. Legacy begins the moment you bless instead of burden. Legacy begins the moment you speak life instead of fear Legacy begins the moment you release the father. Legacy begins the moment you parent from wholeness. Legacy begins the moment you choose love over memory. Legacy begins the moment you rewrite emotional language. Legacy begins the moment you invite God into your motherhood.

You are not just healing a heart; you are healing a generation. You are rewriting the story for people who will never know the weight you carried but will live in the peace you created.

CHAPTER 20

A New Mother Arises — Whole, Calm, and Free

What Healed Motherhood Looks and Feels Like

Healing doesn't just change reactions. It changes **identity**. A woman who once lived in survival mode becomes a woman who lives in freedom. A mother who once carried emotional weight begins to move lightly. A mother who once felt triggered begins to feel grounded.

A mother who once felt overwhelmed begins to feel capable. A mother who once felt shame begins to feel dignity. A mother who once felt resentment begins to feel compassion.

A mother who once feared becoming like the man who did all these things to her now begins to see she was never like him at all.

This chapter is a portrait of the healed mother — the woman God always saw beneath the pain, beneath the exhaustion, beneath the emotional noise, beneath the survival strategies. She is now emerging.

1. She Is Emotionally Present. The healed mother is *here*. Not distracted. Not numb. Not overwhelmed. Not hidden behind survival. She listens with her whole face. She responds with softness. She notices details again: changes in her child's expression, shifts in tone, signs of emotional need, moments that need comfort, opportunities to encourage.

She no longer feels drained by her child's needs. She feels connected to them. Her presence is her power.

2. She Is Calm in Moments That Used to Trigger Her. Triggers lose their sting when wounds are healed. Situations that once caused frustration, panic, resentment, shame, fear, emotional tension. She now invites patience, empathy, clarity, groundedness, emotional maturity.

She pauses naturally. She breathes deeply. She responds thoughtfully. She sees the child's behavior as growth, not challenge. She sees needs as opportunities, not burdens. She sees conflict as something to guide, not fear.

The storm inside her has stilled.

3. She Carries Peace in Her Presence. Peace becomes noticeable. The home feels tranquil. Her voice is gentle. Her energy is stable. Her reactions are predictable. Her emotions feel safe to the child. Her presence becomes a refuge. The child draws near instead of withdrawing. The child expresses emotions instead of hiding them. The child asks questions without fear. The child hugs her more freely. The child trusts her more deeply. Peace is something she carries, not something she chases.

4. She Forgives Herself

Forgiveness toward the man happened earlier. Now it's time for the forgiveness that she didn't even realize she needed: **self-forgiveness.**

A healed mother says, "I didn't know. I didn't mean it. I was overwhelmed. I was hurting. I was unsupported. I was not a bad mother — I was a wounded one." Self-forgiveness breaks internal criticism. It silences shame. It restores dignity.

She no longer uses her past reactions as proof of failure. She sees them as evidence of her need for healing--a need God has now met.

5. She Establishes Emotional Boundaries with the Father. Healing makes boundaries easier. She is no longer triggered by him. She is no longer vulnerable to his inconsistency, affected by his emotional immaturity, intimidated by his presence, manipulated by guilt, or pressured by expectation, destabilized by his choices.

She interacts without tension. She communicates without emotional weight. She decides without fear. She protects herself without apology. The father no longer holds influence over her inner world. Her peace is no longer negotiable.

6. She Becomes the Emotional Anchor of the Home.

Instead of reacting to the child, she becomes the stabilizer, the comforter, the guide, the emotional thermostat, the safe place, the keeper of peace, the spiritual covering. Her stability becomes the child's security. Her consistency becomes the child's safety. Her peace becomes the child's predictability. She becomes what the father never was — not out of pressure, but out of healing.

7. She Enjoys Motherhood Again. Enjoyment returns. She finds joy in small conversations, funny moments, daily routines, shared laughter, shared meals, quiet evenings, unexpected hugs, watching the child grow. The emotional heaviness she once carried is gone. In its place is delight. She begins to see motherhood not as a burden, but as a blessing she is now equipped to cherish.

8. She Sees Herself as God Sees Her. This is the final stage of healing. She no longer sees herself through the lens of wounds, failures, triggers, shame, regret, exhaustion, survival.

She sees her strength, her resilience, her tenderness, her love, her capacity, her growth, her transformation, her anointing, her identity, her spiritual authority. She sees herself as a restored woman, not a broken one. She is a chosen woman, not an abandoned one. She is a healed mother, not a struggling one.

Amen. God's reflection becomes her own.

9. She Becomes a Generational Breaker and Builder

A healed mother breaks old cycle, builds new ones, ends generational trauma, births generational peace, protects generational identity, restores generational blessings, becomes the turning point in her lineage. She writes a new chapter for everyone who comes after her.

Her children and grandchildren will live in the freedom she created. Now, and finally, her legacy is not her pain, it is her healing.

10. She Stands in the Light Her Pain Tried to Hide. The healed mother stands with dignity, confidence, peace, clarity, emotional openness, spiritual strength. She has walked through the valley. She has broken the cycle. She has reclaimed her home. She has reconnected with her child. She has rewritten the emotional language of her household. She has rewritten her lineage. She has become the woman her younger self prayed to be. She is not who she used to be. She is who God always intended. A new mother has arisen whole, calm, and free.

CHAPTER 21

Declarations for Motherhood, Healing, and Legacy

Speaking Truth to Sustain the Freedom God Has Given You

Healing begins in revelation, but it is sustained through declaration. What you speak becomes not only what you believe, but also what you reinforce, what you cultivate, what you live out, and what you pass down.

Declarations establish identity. They seal emotional healing. They fortify spiritual restoration. They break old patterns. They protect new ones. They shape the atmosphere of the home.

Speak these daily, weekly, or whenever your spirit needs alignment. They are written in first-person because healing is personal and intimate.

SECTION 1: Declarations for the Mother's Heart

1. I am healing, and I am whole.
2. I am not defined by the man's choices.
3. I release every emotional weight that is not mine to carry.
4. I refuse to parent through pain — I parent through peace.

5. My heart is soft, steady, and open.

6. My emotions are aligned with truth, not triggers.

7. God is restoring every part of me that was wounded.

8. I give myself grace for the seasons I survived.

9. Shame has no place in me — I walk in dignity.

10. I forgive myself for what I did not know.

11. I am becoming the mother I always needed.

12. I am emotionally grounded and spiritually anchored.

SECTION 2: Declarations Over the Child

1. My child is blessed, loved, and chosen by God.

2. My child is not defined by the father's actions.

3. My child is separate, unique, and divinely designed.

4. I speak peace over their mind and healing over their heart.

5. My child will not inherit the emotional patterns I've broken.

6. My child is secure, confident, and deeply loved.

7. My child is free from every shadow of abandonment.

8. I bless my child's identity, purpose, and destiny.

9. My child carries gifts that will bless generations.

10. My child is my joy — not my reminder.

SECTION 3: Declarations for the Home

1. My home is a sanctuary of peace.

2. My home is free from emotional tension and spiritual

residue.

3. My home is filled with warmth, connection, and laughter.

4. The presence of God fills every room.

5. This home is a place of healing and restoration.

6. Anxiety cannot enter here — peace guards our atmosphere.

7. The enemy has no access to my emotions or my child.

8. My home is protected, covered, and watched over by God.

9. This home will be known for love, calm, and safety.

10. The past has no authority in this house.

SECTION 4: Declarations Over the Mother-Child Relationship

1. Our bond is being restored deeply and safely.

2. My child feels safe with me emotionally.

3. I respond with gentleness, not reaction.

4. I listen with compassion and guide with wisdom.

5. Our relationship grows richer and stronger every day.

6. My healed heart creates a healed childhood.

7. My presence brings comfort and stability.

8. We communicate with trust and clarity.

9. Our connection is protected and strengthened by God.

10. Love flows freely between us.

SECTION 5: Declarations Over Legacy and Generations

1. I am the generational breaker in my family line.

2. What wounded me will not wound the generations after me.

3. The cycle stops with me — and blessing starts with me.

4. My healing changes my bloodline.

5. My children and grandchildren will live in peace I never had.

6. I am planting seeds of emotional health and spiritual strength.

7. My lineage will inherit healing, not trauma.

8. My descendants will experience stability, love, and identity.

9. God is rewriting my family's story through me.

10. I am creating a legacy of wholeness.

SECTION 6: Declarations of Spiritual Authority

1. I partner with God in raising my child.

2. I reject every lie, pattern, and residue from the enemy.

3. I walk in authority, peace, and power.

4. No weapon formed against me or my child will prosper.

5. God's plans for my family will not be delayed or derailed.

6. I stand in spiritual clarity and emotional strength.

7. The Holy Spirit guides my reactions and decisions.

8. I hear God's voice concerning my child.

9. I am not alone — heaven backs my motherhood.

10. I am covered, equipped, and anointed for this assignment.

SECTION 7: A Final Blessing for the Mother

Speak this blessing slowly.
Let each sentence settle into your heart.

"I bless my heart with peace,
my home with calm,
my child with safety,
and my lineage with healing.
I declare that old patterns are broken
and new patterns have begun.
I am restored.
My child is restored.
My home is restored.
My future is restored.
God has rewritten my story,
and I walk forward in freedom,
never again carrying what was not mine.
I am a healed mother,
raising a healed child,
building a healed legacy."

Amen.

CHAPTER 22

When She's Mad at Her Father

People--, even women are often ashamed to admit they're still angry at their birth father. They may be unaware of how much the anger they feel toward their birth father still affects their choices. And now, that woman is a mother. She may now be confused about why the anger resurfaces during motherhood. That's her father and how she feels isn't ideal or Godly so she may be doubleminded when it comes to her father; she is stuck between honoring him and resenting him.

But because of that anger and how she feels about her father it may destine her to marry a man just like him because this anger is not dealt with. Unless whatever in the bloodline is handled, healed, or removed those patterns may have to repeat in her life and in the life of her child. It's spiritual. It must be stopped or removed spiritually, not by just being angry or by will power deciding, "I'm not going to be anything like this."

Even if the natural dad is deceased, elderly, estranged, spiritually broken, imprisoned, in denial, or unhealthy the issues that he walked out that are in the bloodline have to be dealt with. It is very unlikely that your father independently did what he did, lived like he lived in total opposition to the others in his bloodline. Look at the patterns. See them. Map them. Now you know how to pray for yourself. Your deliverance, your healing, is the gift that your own child will inherit. You, healed with ensure that your child will not be mad at you, even if you were mad at your own parent.

Women often think, "That was years ago." "I should be over it." "It doesn't affect me now." "He didn't know better." "He did what he could." Motherhood often **re-triggers** old stories. "Motherhood doesn't erase father-wounds--, it exposes them."

When a woman becomes a mother, she starts asking "Why wasn't I protected like this?" "Why didn't he show up for me like I show up for my children?" "Why did he walk away?" "Why didn't he choose me?" "Why didn't he care?" Her inner child and her present self collide. Motherhood is a mirror, and the mirror reveals cracks. Spiritually, there may be generational assignments against a family that may be time-released to start at marriage, or at pregnancy, or at birth. The goal of the enemy always is to put enmity between couples or even between the father and the child and the child and the father. (Malachi 4).

There are different types of father-wounds. Any child would be angry because their father was absent, or present but emotionally unavailable. If he was abusive, broken, addicted or silent, he won't win any awards with his kids. If he was one of those parents who think you can treat a kid any kind of way and they won't remember it. Not true; eve if they can't verbalize hurts, they will

119

internalize them. And then they'll become the kind of parent that the perpetrator is: kinda lousy. The mother must look well to see what kind of man will father her children, because having a child is no guarantee that he will "change," even if he says he will. So look well, because 'what you see is what you'll get.' And sometimes what you didn't see, didn't look for, didn't look at, or refused to see is also what you will get.

You may have had a present father who was critical, controlling, or inconsistent, still not good, maybe even worse. Or, maybe he left and came back and left again. He gave up. He tried but didn't know how. He lived but wasn't alive in the relationship—any or all of these will provoke a child to anger. Each wound has a different emotional signature that shows up in motherhood.

Fathers, do not provoke your children to wrath; instead, bring them up in the discipline and instruction of the Lord. (Ephesians 6:4)

The New Testament says that we may be angry but we should not sin, but unhealed anger creates hypersensitivity in mothers, emotional withdrawal, fear of repeating history, overcompensation, mistrust toward men, resentment toward male children at times, parenting from a place of protection, not presence, guilt, anxiety, over-functioning, perfectionism, identity confusion.

This is important because a person may not know *why* they're reacting this way. Once they know, once they name it, call it what it is that is not for the purpose of attacking the father; it is the first step to healing.

Forgiveness is not forgetting, but it puts a stop to rehearsing the hurt and it does give the father another chance. Forgiveness does not always mean reconciliation; it may mean that the father cannot resume relationship, but like God towards us, we are not holding anything else against him. Live and let live.

Forgiveness is not pretending that nothing happened or lying saying the person is dead or some other final removal of the person if they are indeed alive.

A man can be a natural father just by biology, but a spiritual father is another whole thing. Ideally, that same man should be **both**, but we have not many fathers. The entire creation is waiting for the Sons of God to arise. Each man, each woman should arise at least in their own homes to become spiritual fathers and mothers, starting with their own offspring. But relationships and marriages are put together in the flesh, by the flesh, for the flesh— too many have no clue if the person who will be the other parent of their child has any spirituality at all even though they are healthy enough to create life and give birth.

But for spiritual fatherhood, thank God that God will step in where natural fathers failed.

> When my father and my mother forsake me, then the Lord will take me up.(Psalm 27:10)

Releasing the father from the throne of judgment. Most women subconsciously sit in the judge's seat over their father for decades. This is dangerous. We should not try or judge or attempt execution against anyone who has hurt us; vengeance is the Lord's. We don't know how much punishment is enough—we really don't and when we nominate someone in condemnation or judgment, we are blind witches asking God to do what God won't do, so the devil steps in to try to enact the evil that you wish or declare on another human. Witches will not inherit the Kingdom of Heaven.

This chapter will help you step down from the judgment seat. Judgement belongs to the Lord. That seat is not your place. Let God who is judge of the whole universe have his seat back. Let go of the emotional contract.

When I was a child, I spake as a child, I understood as a child, I thought as a child: but when I became a man, I put away childish things. (1 Corinthians 13:11)

Stop carrying adult anger for a childhood wound. I see it all the time. Shall we be led by the Holy Spirit or by our old emotions? Do you want your child to function that way? They will; because they will see that's how you handle yourself. Therefore, you must stop mothering through the lens of old pain.

Now that you are all grown up take a sober look at your own father and ask the Lord if you should still be angry with your biological father. When you look deeper and listen closely, the Holy Spirit will tell you things about your father, your family, your foundation, your ancestors, even your bloodline. When you are mature enough to ask all this and listen and hear and then also do something about it, you not only will heal yourself, you will heal your bloodline. That healing will bless your child, your future and your legacy. And it will heal you of anger when you realize there may have been some forces at play that your natural father may not have seen, been aware of, or had any clue how to fight them.

At some point in your life you have to look back and see your parents as PEOPLE, not just as parents. With all due respect…

Perhaps your dad didn't know anything about spiritual things or how to pray or deal with those things. This could be why he behaved this way toward your mother and by extension, toward you. Can you now see your own father that you may be angry with as a mirror as to why you think like you do or do as you do? So, don't remain angry with your natural father because he behaved in the natural the way that spiritual things demanded that he act out and he had no ability to fight it.

In closing: Man, fathers and future fathers, women want to celebrate you and show your children how to honor you, but if you are not present and you do nothing honorable, how can we? How shall we? We want to avoid the curse, don't you? you want your children to avoid the curse, right? With all that is in you, fight: never turn away from your father and never turn away from your child.

And he shall turn the heart of the fathers to the children, and the heart of the children to their fathers, lest I come and smite the earth with a curse. (Malachi 4:6)

Dear Reader

Thank you for acquiring and reading, this book. I pray it brings healing and deliverance for yourself, your children, your entire bloodline.

In the Name of Jesus.

Shalom,

Dr. Marlene Miles

This is book 1 of a 3-book set:

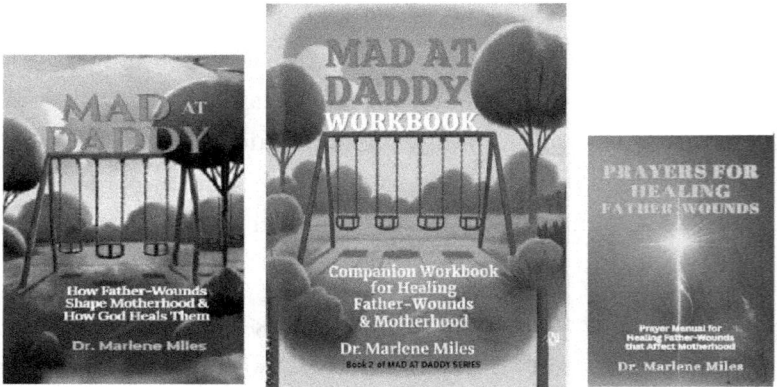

MAD AT DADDY: *How Father-Wounds Shape Motherhood & How God Heals Them*

MAD AT DADDY Workbook: *Companion Workbook for Healing Father-Wounds*

PRAYERS FOR HEALING FATHER WOUNDS: *Prayer Manual*

Prayerbooks by this author

This title is part of a three-part course. The man book, the Workbook & the prayer manual.

FAKE FRIENDS: *Prayers Against Betrayers*

HOLIDAY WARFARE Prayer Manual (humorous) Surviving Family Gatherings All Year Long (without catching a case)

SOUL TIE Prayer Manual (The)   Part of a 3-part series including a workbook.

MAD at DADDY Prayer Manual – part of a 3-part series including a workbook.

Healing the Sibling & Relative Wound Prayer Manual

Healing the Father-Son Wound Prayer Manual

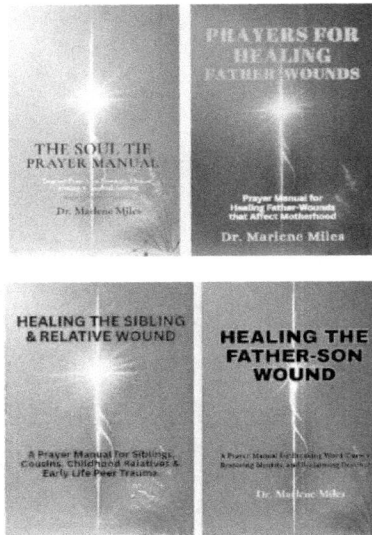

Prayers Against Barrenness: *For Success in Business and Life*

Breaking Curses of the Mother Prayer Manual Breaking the unintentional word curses of my mother. (Includes Warfare Prayer section.)

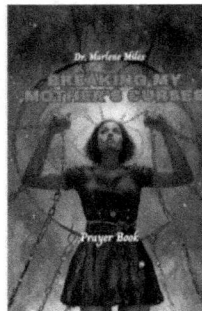

While most books by this author have prayer points either throughout the book or at the end, there are some books that are only prayers. You just open up the book and pray.

Prayers Against Barrenness: *For Success in Business and Life*

Fruit of the Womb: *Prayers Against Barrenness*

Beauty Curses, *Warfare Prayers Against*
https://a.co/d/5Xlc20M

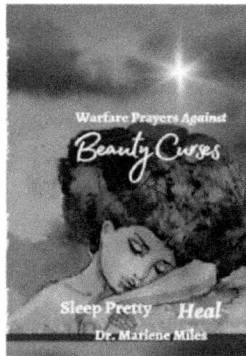

Courts of Marriage: Prayers for Marriage in the Courts of Heaven *(prayerbook)* https://a.co/d/cNAdgAq

Courtroom Warfare @ Midnight *(prayerbook)*
https://a.co/d/5fc7Qdp

Demonic Cobwebs *(prayerbook)* https://a.co/d/fp9Oa2H

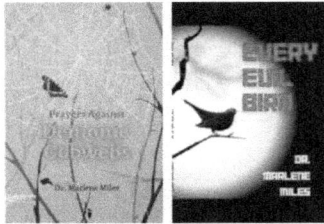

Every Evil Bird https://a.co/d/hF1kh1O

Gates of Thanksgiving

Praise Waits for Thee in Zion

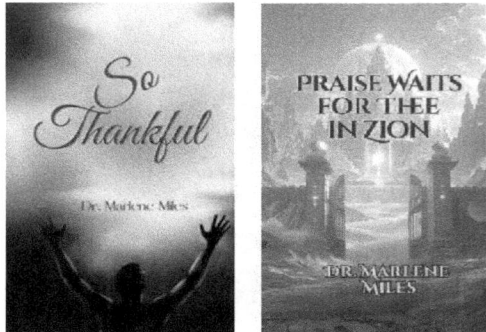

So Thankful https://a.co/d/aePABdZ

Spirits of Death, Hell & the Grave, Pass Over Me and My House

Throne of Grace: Courtroom Prayer

Warfare Prayer Against Poverty
https://a.co/d/bZ61lYu

Other books by this author

200 RED FLAGS: THE TRACK IS NOT SAFE
How to spot red flags in relationships, especially in dating and romantic connections. https://a.co/d/ckyuqmb

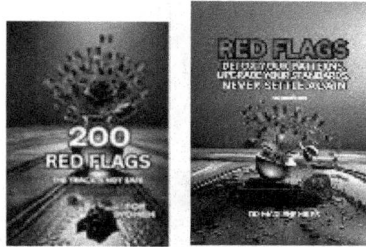

Also. the **RED FLAGS** Workbook. Full size, ample room to write. Have a RED FLAG party with your friends and conquer relationship problems.

AK: The Adventures of the Agape Kid

Already Married in the Spirit: *Why You May Not Be Married in the Natural*

AMONG SOME THIEVES https://a.co/d/dkYT4ZV

Ancestral Powers

Anti-Marriage, *The Spirit of*

Backstabbers https://a.co/d/gi8iBxf

Barrenness, *Prayers Against* https://a.co/d/feUltIs

Battlefield of Marriage, *The*

Beware of the Dog: Prayers Against Dogs in the Dream.

Bless Your Food: *Let the Dining Table be Undefiled*

Blindsided: *Has the Old Man Bewitched You?*
https://a.co/d/5O2fLLR

Break Free from Collective Captivity

Broken Spirits & Dry Bones

By Means of a Whorish Father

Caged Life: Get Out Alive!

https://a.co/d/bwPbksX

Casting Down Imaginations

Churchzilla, The Wanna-Be, Supposed-to-be Bride of Christ

Demonic Cobwebs (prayerbook)

Demonic Time Bombs

Demons Hate Questions

Devil Loves Trauma, *The*

Devil Weapons: Unforgiveness, Bitterness,...

The Devourers: Thieves of Darkness 2

Do Not Swear by the Moon

Don't Refuse Me, Lord (4 book series)

https://a.co/d/idP34LG

Dream Defilement

The Emptiers: *Thieves of Darkness, 1*
https://a.co/d/5I4n5mc

Evil Touch

Failed Assignment

Fantasy Spirit Spouse https://a.co/d/hW7oYbX

FAT Demons (The): *Breaking Demonic Curses*
https://a.co/d/4kP8wV1

The Fold (5-book series)

- The Fold (Book 1)
- Name Your Seed (Book 2)
- The Poor Attitudes of Money (3)
- Do Not Orphan Your Seed (4)
- For the Sake of the Gospel (5)
- My Sowing Journal

Gang Ups: Touch Not God's Anointed

Getting Rid of Evil Spiritual Food

https://a.co/d/i2L3WYQ

got HEALING? Verses for Life

got LOVE? Verses for Life

got HOPE? Verses for Life

got money?   https://a.co/d/g2av41N

Has My Soul Been Sold? https://a.co/d/dyB8hhA

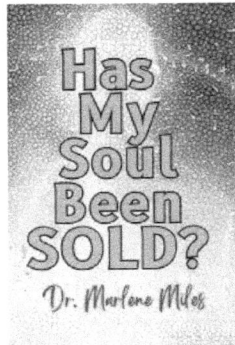

Here Come the Horns: *Skilled to Destroy*
https://a.co/d/cZiNnkP

Hidden Sins: Hidden Iniquity

https://a.co/d/4Mth0wa

How to Dental Assist

How to Dental Assist2: Be Productive, Not Wasteful

How to STOP Being a Blind Witch or Warlock

I Take It Back

Legacy

Let Me Have A Dollar's Worth
https://a.co/d/h8F8XgE

Let Them Come Up & Worship
https://a.co/d/3yEAPMW

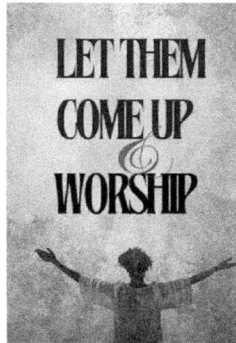

LET THEM COME UP & WORSHIP

Level the Playing Field

Living for the NOW of God

Lose My Location https://a.co/d/crD6mV9

Love Breaks Your Heart

Made Perfect In Love

Mammon https://a.co/d/29yhMG7

Man Safari, *The*

Marriage Ed. Rules of Engagement & Marriage

Made Perfect in Love

Money Hunters: Beware of Those

Money on the Altar https://a.co/d/4EqJ2Nr

Mulberry Tree, *The* https://a.co/d/9nR9rRb

Motherboard (The) - *Soul Prosperity Series*

Name Your Seed

Occupy: *Until I Return* https://a.co/d/bZ7ztUy

Opponent, Adversary, or Enemy?: Fight The Right Battle with the Right Weapons

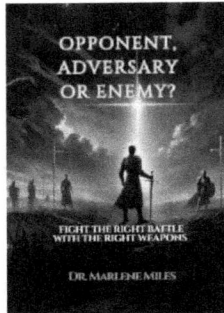

Plantation Souls

Players Gonna Play

Portals: Shut the Front Door: Prayers to Close Evil Portals.

Power Money: Nine Times the Tithe

https://a.co/d/gRt41gy

The Power to Get Wealth https://a.co/d/e4ub4Ov

Powers Above

The Robe, Part 1, The Lessons of Joseph

The Robe, Part II, The Lessons of Joseph

Seasons of Grief

Seasons of Waiting

Seasons of War

Second Marriage, Third--, *Any Marriage*

https://a.co/d/6m6GN4N

Seducing Spirits: Idolatry & Whoredoms

https://a.co/d/4Jq4WEs

Shut the Front Door: *Prayers to Close Portals*
https://a.co/d/cH4TWJj

Sift You Like Wheat

Six Men Short: What Has Happened to all the Men?

SLAVE

Sleep Afflictions & Really Bad Dreams
https://a.co/d/f8sDmgv

Soul Prosperity soul prosperity series 3

https://a.co/d/5p8YvCN

Souls Captivity soul prosperity series 2

The Spirit of Anti-Marriage

The Spirit of Poverty https://a.co/d/abV2o2e

Spiritual Thieves https://a.co/d/eqPPz33

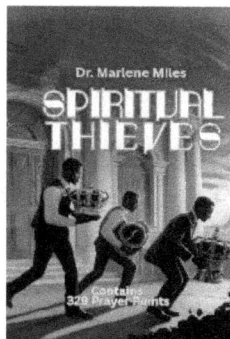

StarStruck- Triangular Power series.

SUNBLOCK- Triangular Power series.

The Swallowers: *Thieves of Darkness*, 3

Take It Back

This Is NOT That: How to Keep Demons from Coming at You

Time Is of the Essence

Too Many Wives: *Why You Have Lady Problems*

Tormenting Spirits   https://a.co/d/dAogEJf

Toxic Souls

Triangular Power *(series)*, Powers Above, SUNBLOCK, Do Not Swear by the Moon, STARSTRUCK

Unbreak My Heart: *Don't Let Me Die*

Uncontested Doom

Unguarded Hours, *The*

Unseen Life, *The* (forthcoming)

Upgrade: How to Get Out of Survival Mode Toxic Souls (Book 2 of series) , Legacy (Book 3 of series)

The Wasters: *Thieves of Darkness*, Bk 2
https://a.co/d/bUvI9Jo

What Have You to Declare? What Do You Have With You from Where You've Been?

When I Was A Child, *I Prayed As a Child*

When the Devourer is Rebuked

https://a.co/d/1HVv8oq

WTH? Get Me Out of This Hell
https://a.co/d/a7WBGJh

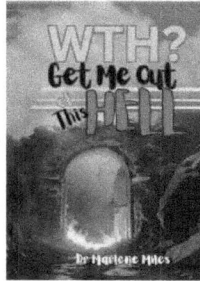

The Wilderness Romance *(series)* This series is about conducting a Godly relationship and marriage with someone who is a Wilderness person. It is about how to recognize it and navigate through it. These books are about how not to get caught up in such.

- *The Social Wilderness*
- *The Sexual Wilderness*
- *The Spiritual Wilderness*

Other Series

The Fold (a series on Godly finances)
https://a.co/d/4hz3unj

Soul Prosperity Series https://a.co/d/bz2M42q

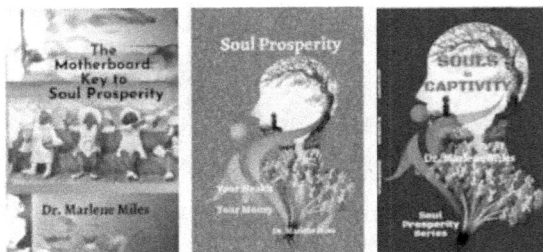

Spirit Spouse books

https://a.co/d/9VehDSo

https://a.co/d/97sKOwm

Battlefield of Marriage, The

https://a.co/d/eUDzizO

Players Gonna Play

https://a.co/d/2hzGw3N

Sent Spirit Spouse (can someone send you a spirit spouse? This book is not yet released.)

Matters of the Heart, Made Perfect in Love
https://a.co/d/70MQW3O , Love Breaks Your Heart
https://a.co/d/4KvuQLZ, Unbreak My Heart
https://a.co/d/84ceZ6M Broken Spirits & Dry Bones
https://a.co/d/e6iedNP

Thieves of Darkness series

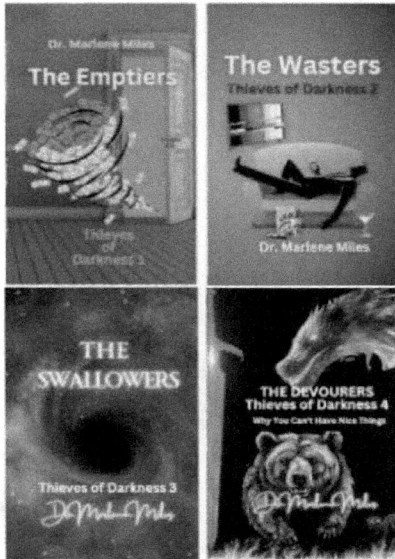

The Emptiers https://a.co/d/heio0dO

The Wasters https://a.co/d/5TG1iNQ

The Swallowers https://a.co/d/1jWhM6G

The Devourers: Why We Can't Have Nice Things
https://a.co/d/87Tejbf

Spiritual Thieves

Triangular Powers https://a.co/d/aUCjAWC

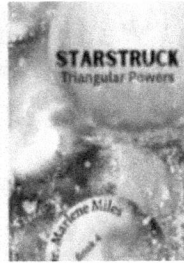

WE GET ALONG, RIGHT? *Compatibility Reality for Couples*

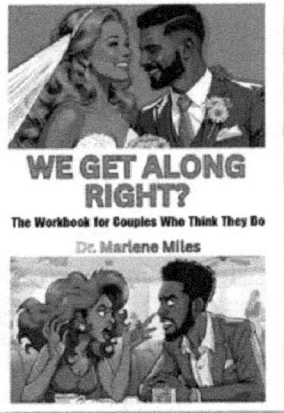

Companion Workbook: **WE GET ALONG, RIGHT?** *The Workbook for Couples Who Think They Do*

The Wilderness Romance (series on relationships – nonfiction)

The Wilderness Romance *(series)* This series is about conducting a Godly relationship and marriage with someone who is a Wilderness person. It is about how to recognize it and navigate through it. These books are about how not to get caught up in such.

- *The Social Wilderness*
- *The Sexual Wilderness*
- *The Spiritual Wilderness*

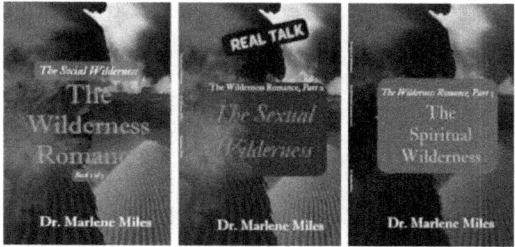

Upgrade (series) *How to Get Out of Survival Mode*
https://a.co/d/aTERhXO

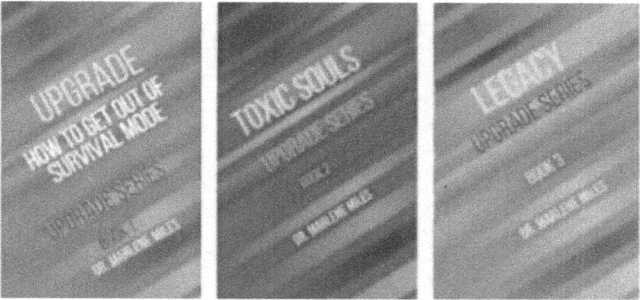

About the Author

Dr. Marlene Miles writes from a place of lived experience, personal healing, and a deep desire to see others whole. She knows what it feels like to carry painful words, to struggle with identity, and to long for God to rewrite the story. Through her journey, she discovered the power of prayer, reflection, and Scripture in transforming the heart.

Today, she shares those revelations with others—helping them break cycles, heal emotionally, and discover the beauty of God's truth over their lives. Her ministry flows with gentleness, honesty, and a prophetic sensitivity that reaches hearts right where they are.

Her calling is to help the broken become whole, the weary find rest, and the wounded step into purpose. Every book she writes is an offering of healing, hope, and freedom.

www.ingramcontent.com/pod-product-compliance
Lightning Source LLC
LaVergne TN
LVHW052029080426
835513LV00018B/2245